My Daily Gift
100 Promises for your every need

Copyright© 2014 by Inprov, Ltd.
ISBN: 978-0-9914820-1-6

For further information, write Inprov, at:
2150 E Continental Blvd, Southlake. TX 76092

All rights reserved. No part of this publication may be reproduced, stored in a retrieval system or transmitted in any form or by any means, electronic, mechanical, photocopying, recording or otherwise, without the prior written permission of the copyright's owners.

Scripture quotations marked (NIV) are taken from THE HOLY BIBLE, NEW INTERNATIONAL VERSION®, NIV® Copyright © 1973, 1978, 1984, 2011 by Biblica, Inc.™ Used by permission. All rights reserved worldwide.

Scripture quotations marked (NLT) are taken from the Holy Bible, New Living Translation, copyright © 1996, 2004, 2007 by Tyndale House Foundation. Used by permission of Tyndale House Publishers, Inc., Carol Stream, Illinois 60188. All rights reserved.

Scripture quotations marked (NKJV) are taken from the New King James Version®. Copyright © 1982 by Thomas Nelson, Inc. Used by permission. All rights reserved.

Scripture quotations marked The Message are taken from The Message. Copyright © 1993, 1994, 1995, 1996, 2000, 2001, 2002. Used by permission of NavPress Publishing Group.

Scripture quotations marked (AMP) are taken from the Amplified® Bible, Copyright © 1954, 1958, 1962, 1964, 1965, 1987 by The Lockman Foundation. Used by permission.

Scripture quotations marked (NASB) are taken from the NEW AMERICAN STANDARD BIBLE®, Copyright © 1960,1962,1963,1968,1971,1972,1973,1975,1977,1995 by The Lockman Foundation. Used by permission.

Scripture quotations marked (CEV) are taken from the Contemporary English Version®.

Copyright © 1995 American Bible Society. All rights reserved.

Scripture quotations marked (NKJV) are taken from the New King James Version®. Copyright © 1982 by Thomas Nelson, Inc. Used by permission. All rights reserved.

my Daily Gift

100 Promises
for your every need

❧ Contents ❧

my Daily Gift of…

Introduction

My Daily Gift . . . was created with the hope of you recognizing and receiving the gifts God promises you in His Word—gifts of restoration, healing, favor, provision and protection—because it is our privilege as believers to claim the gifts that are already in Christ.

No matter what you are going through in life—joy or sorrow, pain or blessing—everything you need in order to live a life that is fulfilling is already yours if you are a believer in Jesus Christ (see 2 Peter 1:3).

When you need patience, Jesus gives patience. When you need rest, Jesus gives rest. When you need victory and strength, Jesus gives victory and strength. When you are discouraged, Jesus gives encouragement. When you need wisdom, Jesus gives wisdom.

All of the gifts we can enjoy are received through the gift of Jesus Himself. By going to the cross for our sins, He gave us the opportunity to know the Father and to have eternal life. Not because of anything we've given Him, but because of the gift of Jesus, His Son, to us.

The 100 gifts detailed in the pages ahead are just the beginning. We encourage you to use this book as a launching point into all that God's Word has for you in the gift of Jesus Himself.

Absolution

*(a formal cancellation of the debt incurred
by sin or obligation)*

And I will forgive their wickedness, and I will never again remember their sins. HEBREWS 8:12 NLT

Once we, too, were foolish and disobedient. We were misled and became slaves to many lusts and pleasures. Our lives were full of evil and envy, and we hated each other. But—"When God our Savior revealed his kindness and love, he saved us, not because of the righteous things we had done, but because of his mercy. He washed away our sins, giving us a new birth and new life through the Holy Spirit." TITUS 3:3–5 NLT

And being made perfect, he became the author of eternal salvation unto all them that obey him . . . HEBREWS 5:9 KJV

Jesus said to the woman, "Your faith has saved you; go in peace." LUKE 7:50 NIV

He personally carried our sins in his body on the cross so that we can be dead to sin and live for what is right. By his wounds you are healed. 1 PETER 2:24 NLT

The next day he saw Jesus coming toward him, and said, "Behold, the Lamb of God, who takes away the sin of the world!" JOHN 1:29 ESV

Abundance

(more than enough; plenty)

Moses said this about the tribes of Joseph: "May their land be blessed by the LORD with the precious gift of dew from the heavens and water from beneath the earth; with the rich fruit that grows in the sun, and the rich harvest produced each month; with the finest crops of the ancient mountains, and the abundance from the everlasting hills; with the best gifts of the earth and its bounty, and the favor of the one who appeared in the burning bush. May these blessings rest on Joseph's head, crowning the brow of the prince among his brothers." DEUTERONOMY 33:13–16 NLT

How abundant are the good things that you have stored up for those who fear you, that you bestow in the sight of all, on those who take refuge in you. PSALM 31:19 NIV

"But we have only five loaves of bread and two fish!" they answered. "Bring them here," he said. Then he told the people to sit down on the grass. Jesus took the five loaves and two fish, looked up toward heaven, and blessed them. Then, breaking the loaves into pieces, he gave the bread to the disciples, who distributed it to the people. They all ate as much as they wanted, and afterward, the disciples picked up twelve baskets of leftovers. About 5,000 men were fed that day, in addition to all the women and children! MATTHEW 14:17–21 NLT

To those who use well what they are given, even more will be given, and they will have an abundance. But from those who do nothing, even what little they have will be taken away. MATTHEW 25:29 NLT

"Yes," Jesus replied, "and I assure you that everyone who has given up house or brothers or sisters or mother or father or children or property, for my sake and for the Good News, will receive now in return a hundred times as many houses, brothers, sisters, mothers, children, and property—along with persecution. And in the world to come that person will have eternal life." MARK 10:29–30 NLT

The thief comes only to steal and kill and destroy; I came that they may have life, and have *it* abundantly. JOHN 10:10 NASB

When he had finished speaking, he said to Simon, "Put out into deep water, and let down the nets for a catch. "Simon answered, "Master, we've worked hard all night and haven't caught anything. But because you say so, I will let down the nets." When they had done so, they caught such a large number of fish that their nets began to break. So they signaled their partners in the other boat to come and help them, and they came and filled both boats so full that they began to sink. LUKE 5:4–7 NIV

Now this *I say*, he who sows sparingly will also reap sparingly, and he who sows bountifully will also reap bountifully. Each one *must* do just as he has purposed in his heart, not grudgingly or under compulsion, for God loves a cheerful giver. And God is able to make all grace abound to you, so that always having all sufficiency in everything, you may have an abundance for every good deed . . .
2 CORINTHIANS 9:6–8 NASB

∞ Day 3 ∞

Acceptance

(to receive; to find worthy)

For on my holy mountain, the great mountain of Israel, says the Sovereign LORD, the people of Israel will someday worship me, and I will accept them. There I will require that you bring me all your offerings and choice gifts and sacrifices. EZEKIEL 20:40 NLT

When he prays to God, he will be accepted. And God will receive him with joy and restore him to good standing. JOB 33:26 NLT

"Everyone who acknowledges me publicly here on earth, I will also acknowledge before my Father in heaven." MATTHEW 10:32 NLT

Then Peter began to speak: "I now realize how true it is that God does not show favoritism but accepts from every nation the one who fears him and does what is right." ACTS 10:34–35 NIV

And this hope will not lead to disappointment. For we know how dearly God loves us, because he has given us the Holy Spirit to fill our hearts with his love. ROMANS 5:5 NLT

Therefore, accept each other just as Christ has accepted you so that God will be given glory. ROMANS 15:7 NLT

Even before he made the world, God loved us and chose us in Christ to be holy and without fault in his eyes. God decided in advance to adopt us into his own family by bringing us to himself through Jesus Christ. This is what he wanted to do, and it gave him great pleasure. So we praise God for the glorious grace he has poured out on us who belong to his dear Son. EPHESIANS 1:4–6 NLT

For in Scripture it says: "See, I lay a stone in Zion, a chosen and precious cornerstone, and the one who trusts in him will never be put to shame." 1 PETER 2:6 NIV

"…the one who
trusts in him will never
be put to *shame*."

Acquittal

*(cleared of a charge; released from a duty
or obligation; declared not guilty)*

Who can discern *his* errors? Acquit me of hidden *faults*. Also keep back Your servant from presumptuous sins; Let them not rule over me; Then I will be blameless, And I shall be acquitted of great transgression. PSALM 19:12–13 NASB

Declare me not guilty, O LORD my God, for you give justice. Don't let my enemies laugh about me in my troubles. PSALM 35:24 NLT

"And I tell you this, you must give an account on judgment day for every idle word you speak. The words you say will either acquit you or condemn you." MATTHEW 12:36–37 NLT

"This is how much God loved the world: He gave his Son, his one and only Son. And this is why: so that no one need be destroyed; by believing in him, anyone can have a whole and lasting life. God didn't go to all the trouble of sending his Son merely to point an accusing finger, telling the world how bad it was. He came to help, to put the world right again. Anyone who trusts in him is acquitted; anyone who refuses to trust him has long since been under the death sentence without knowing it. And why? Because of that person's failure to believe in the one-of-a-kind Son of God when introduced to him." JOHN 3:16–18 MSG

They said, "Believe in the Lord Jesus, and you will be saved, you and your household." ACTS 16:31 NASB

Adoption

(to take into one's own family)

For my father and my mother have forsaken me, but the LORD will take me in. PSALM 27:10 ESV

But to all who believed him and accepted him, he gave the right to become children of God. JOHN 1:12 NLT

So you have not received a spirit that makes you fearful slaves. Instead, you received God's Spirit when he adopted you as his own children. Now we call him, "Abba, Father." ROMANS 8:15 NLT

"And I will be your Father, and you will be my sons and daughters, says the LORD Almighty." 2 CORINTHIANS 6:18 NLT

And that's the way it was with us before Christ came. We were like children; we were slaves to the basic spiritual principles of this world. But when the right time came, God sent his Son, born of a woman, subject to the law. God sent him to buy freedom for us who were slaves to the law, so that he could adopt us as his very own children. And because we are his children, God has sent the Spirit of his Son into our hearts, prompting us to call out, "Abba, Father." Now you are no longer a slave but God's own child. And since you are his child, God has made you his heir. GALATIANS 4:3–7 NLT

Even before he made the world, God loved us and chose us in Christ to be holy and without fault in his eyes. God decided in advance

∽ *continued* ∽

to adopt us into his own family by bringing us to himself through Jesus Christ. This is what he wanted to do, and it gave him great pleasure. EPHESIANS 1:4–5 NLT

See what great love the Father has lavished on us, that we should be called children of God! And that is what we are! The reason the world does not know us is that it did not know him. Dear friends, now we are children of God, and what we will be has not yet been made known. But we know that when Christ appears, we shall be like him, for we shall see him as he is. All who have this hope in him purify themselves, just as he is pure. 1 JOHN 3:1–3 NIV

See what *great love* the
Father has lavished on us,
that we should be called
children of God!

Affirmation

(something declared to be true)

Let your servants see what you're best at—the ways you rule and bless your children. And let the loveliness of our Lord, our God, rest on us, confirming the work that we do. Oh, yes. Affirm the work that we do! PSALM 90:16–17 MSG

GOD, teach me lessons for living so I can stay the course. Give me insight so I can do what you tell me—my whole life one long, obedient response. Guide me down the road of your commandments; I love traveling this freeway! Give me a bent for your words of wisdom, and not for piling up loot. Divert my eyes from toys and trinkets, invigorate me on the pilgrim way. Affirm your promises to me— promises made to all who fear you. Deflect the harsh words of my critics—but what you say is always so good. See how hungry I am for your counsel; preserve my life through your righteous ways! PSALM 119:33–40 MSG

For all who are led by the Spirit of God are children of God. So you have not received a spirit that makes you fearful slaves. Instead, you received God's Spirit when he adopted you as his own children. Now we call him, "Abba, Father." For his Spirit joins with our spirit to affirm that we are God's children. And since we are his children, we are his heirs. In fact, together with Christ we are heirs of God's glory. But if we are to share his glory, we must also share his suffering. ROMANS 8:14–17 NLT

For no matter how many promises God has made, they are "Yes" in Christ. And so through him the "Amen" is spoken by us to the glory of God. Now it is God who makes both us and you stand firm in Christ. He anointed us, set his seal of ownership on us, and put his Spirit in our hearts as a deposit, guaranteeing what is to come. 2 CORINTHIANS 1:20–22 NIV

It's in Christ that you, once you heard the truth and believed it (this Message of your salvation), found yourselves home free—signed, sealed, and delivered by the Holy Spirit. This signet from God is the first installment on what's coming, a reminder that we'll get everything God has planned for us, a praising and glorious life. EPHESIANS 1:13–14 MSG

Let us hold tightly without wavering to the hope we affirm, for God can be trusted to keep his promise. HEBREWS 10:23 NLT

We have everything we need to live a life that pleases God. It was all given to us by God's own power, when we learned that he had invited us to share in his wonderful goodness. God made great and marvelous promises, so that his nature would become part of us. Then we could escape our evil desires and the corrupt influences of this world . . . My friends, you must do all you can to show that God has really chosen and selected you. If you keep on doing this, you won't stumble and fall. Then our Lord and Savior Jesus Christ will give you a glorious welcome into his kingdom that will last forever. 2 PETER 1:3–4, 10–11 CEV

Anointing

(to rub oil on; to make holy; to dedicate)

The LORD is my shepherd, I lack nothing. He makes me lie down in green pastures, he leads me beside quiet waters, he refreshes my soul. He guides me along the right paths for his name's sake. Even though I walk through the darkest valley, I will fear no evil, for you are with me; your rod and your staff, they comfort me. You prepare a table before me in the presence of my enemies. You anoint my head with oil; my cup overflows. Surely your goodness and love will follow me all the days of my life, and I will dwell in the house of the LORD forever. **PSALM 23:1–6 NIV**

You love justice and hate evil. Therefore God, your God, has anointed you, pouring out the oil of joy on you more than on anyone else. **PSALM 45:7 NLT**

The Spirit of the Sovereign LORD is on me, because the LORD has anointed me to proclaim good news to the poor. He has sent me to bind up the brokenhearted, to proclaim freedom for the captives and release from darkness for the prisoners . . . **ISAIAH 61:1 NIV**

As for you, the anointing you received from him remains in you, and you do not need anyone to teach you. But as his anointing teaches you about all things and as that anointing is real, not counterfeit—just as it has taught you, remain in him. **1 JOHN 2:27 NIV**

Answers

(a reply; a solution to a problem or request)

The LORD has heard my plea; the LORD will answer my prayer.
PSALM 6:9 NLT

You who answer prayer, to you all people will come. PSALM 65:2 NIV

He will respond to the prayer of the destitute; he will not despise
their plea. PSALM 102:17 NIV

People of Zion, who live in Jerusalem, you will weep no more. How
gracious he will be when you cry for help! As soon as he hears, he
will answer you. ISAIAH 30:19 NIV

The LORD says, "I was ready to respond, but no one asked for
help. I was ready to be found, but no one was looking for me.
I said, 'Here I am, here I am!' to a nation that did not call on my
name." ISAIAH 65:1 NLT

It will also come to pass that before they call, I will answer; and
while they are still speaking, I will hear. ISAIAH 65:24 NASB

Then Jesus said to the disciples, "Have faith in God. I tell you
the truth, you can say to this mountain, 'May you be lifted up and
thrown into the sea,' and it will happen. But you must really believe
it will happen and have no doubt in your heart. I tell you, you can
pray for anything, and if you believe that you've received it, it will
be yours." MARK 11:22–24 NLT

You can ask for anything in my name, and I will do it, so that the Son can bring glory to the Father. Yes, ask me for anything in my name, and I will do it! JOHN 14:13–14 NLT

In that day you will no longer ask me anything. Very truly I tell you, my Father will give you whatever you ask in my name. Until now you have not asked for anything in my name. Ask and you will receive, and your joy will be complete. JOHN 16:23–24 NIV

Dear friends, if our hearts do not condemn us, we have confidence before God and receive from him anything we ask, because we keep his commands and do what pleases him. And this is his command: to believe in the name of his Son, Jesus Christ, and to love one another as he commanded us. The one who keeps God's commands lives in him, and he in them. And this is how we know that he lives in us: We know it by the Spirit he gave us. 1 JOHN 3:21–24 NIV

This is the confidence we have in approaching God: that if we ask anything according to his will, he hears us. And if we know that he hears us—whatever we ask—we know that we have what we asked of him. 1 JOHN 5:14–15 NIV

Approval

(to have a favorable opinion; to deem worthy)

Open up before God, keep nothing back; he'll do whatever needs to be done: He'll validate your life in the clear light of day and stamp you with approval at high noon. PSALM 37:5–6 MSG

And may the Lord our God show us his approval and make our efforts successful. Yes, make our efforts successful! PSALM 90:17 NLT

The LORD approves of those who are good, but he condemns those who plan wickedness. PROVERBS 12:2 NLT

When God approves of your life, even your enemies will end up shaking your hand. PROVERBS 16:7 MSG

For the Kingdom of God is not a matter of what we eat or drink, but of living a life of goodness and peace and joy in the Holy Spirit. If you serve Christ with this attitude, you will please God, and others will approve of you, too. ROMANS 14:17–18 NLT

First, I hear that there are divisions among you when you meet as a church, and to some extent I believe it. But, of course, there must be divisions among you so that you who have God's approval will be recognized! 1 CORINTHIANS 11:18–19 NLT

For it is not he who commends himself that is approved, but he whom the Lord commends. 2 CORINTHIANS 10:18 NASB

Obviously, I'm not trying to win the approval of people, but of God. If pleasing people were my goal, I would not be Christ's servant. GALATIANS 1:10 NLT

For we speak as messengers approved by God to be entrusted with the Good News. Our purpose is to please God, not people. He alone examines the motives of our hearts. Never once did we try to win you with flattery, as you well know. And God is our witness that we were not pretending to be your friends just to get your money! As for human praise, we have never sought it from you or anyone else. 1 THESSALONIANS 2:4–6 NLT

Work hard so you can present yourself to God and receive his approval. Be a good worker, one who does not need to be ashamed and who correctly explains the word of truth. 2 TIMOTHY 2:15 NLT

Be a *good worker,* one who does not need to be ashamed and who correctly explains *the word of truth.*

Atonement

(to make amends; the redeeming of mankind)

But he was pierced for our transgressions, he was crushed for our iniquities; the punishment that brought us peace was on him, and by his wounds we are healed. ISAIAH 53:5 NIV

"He is the one all the prophets testified about, saying that everyone who believes in him will have their sins forgiven through his name." ACTS 10:43 NLT

... and all are justified freely by his grace through the redemption that came by Christ Jesus. God presented Christ as a sacrifice of atonement, through the shedding of his blood to be received by faith. He did this to demonstrate his righteousness, because in his forbearance he had left the sins committed beforehand unpunished—he did it to demonstrate his righteousness at the present time, so as to be just and the one who justifies those who have faith in Jesus. ROMANS 3:24–26 NIV

My old self has been crucified with Christ. It is no longer I who live, but Christ lives in me. So I live in this earthly body by trusting in the Son of God, who loved me and gave himself for me. GALATIANS 2:20 NLT

He himself is the sacrifice that atones for our sins—and not only our sins but the sins of all the world. 1 JOHN 2:2 NLT

This is love: not that we loved God, but that he loved us and sent his Son as an atoning sacrifice for our sins. 1 JOHN 4:10 NIV

Therefore he is able to save completely those who come to God through him, because he always lives to intercede for them. Such a high priest truly meets our need—one who is holy, blameless, pure, set apart from sinners, exalted above the heavens. Unlike the other high priests, he does not need to offer sacrifices day after day, first for his own sins, and then for the sins of the people. He sacrificed for their sins once for all when he offered himself. For the law appoints as high priests men in all their weakness; but the oath, which came after the law, appointed the Son, who has been made perfect forever. HEBREWS 7:25–28 NIV

Just as people are destined to die once, and after that to face judgment, so Christ was sacrificed once to take away the sins of many; and he will appear a second time, not to bear sin, but to bring salvation to those who are waiting for him. HEBREWS 9:27–28 NIV

He is the faithful witness to these things, the first to rise from the dead, and the ruler of all the kings of the world. All glory to him who loves us and has freed us from our sins by shedding his blood for us. REVELATION 1:5 NLT

Authority

(a delegation of power; the right to give commands, take action, or make decisions)

When the crowd saw this, they were filled with awe; and they praised God, who had given such authority to man. MATTHEW 9:8 NIV

Jesus called his twelve disciples to him and gave them authority to drive out impure spirits and to heal every disease and sickness. MATTHEW 10:1 NIV

Then Jesus came to them and said, "All authority in heaven and on earth has been given to me. Therefore go and make disciples of all nations, baptizing them in the name of the Father and of the Son and of the Holy Spirit, and teaching them to obey everything I have commanded you. And surely I am with you always, to the very end of the age." MATTHEW 28:18–20 NIV

One day Jesus called together his twelve disciples and gave them power and authority to cast out all demons and to heal all diseases. Then he sent them out to tell everyone about the Kingdom of God and to heal the sick. LUKE 9:1–2 NLT

Behold, I have given you authority to tread on serpents and scorpions, and over all the power of the enemy, and nothing shall hurt you. LUKE 10:19 ESV

Everyone must submit to governing authorities. For all authority comes from God, and those in positions of authority have been placed there by God. So anyone who rebels against authority is rebelling against what God has instituted, and they will be punished. ROMANS 13:1–2 NLT

Look at the obvious facts. Those who say they belong to Christ must recognize that we belong to Christ as much as they do. I may seem to be boasting too much about the authority given to us by the Lord. But our authority builds you up; it doesn't tear you down. So I will not be ashamed of using my authority. 2 CORINTHIANS 10:7–8 NLT

But our authority
builds you up;
it doesn't tear
you down.

Blessing

(gift of divine favor)

All these blessings will come on you and accompany you if you obey the LORD your God: You will be blessed in the city and blessed in the country. The fruit of your womb will be blessed, and the crops of your land and the young of your livestock—the calves of your herds and the lambs of your flocks. Your basket and your kneading trough will be blessed. You will be blessed when you come in and blessed when you go out. DEUTERONOMY 28:2–6 NIV

See, I set before you today life and prosperity, death and destruction. For I command you today to love the LORD your God, to walk in obedience to him, and to keep his commands, decrees and laws; then you will live and increase, and the LORD your God will bless you in the land you are entering to possess.
DEUTERONOMY 30:15–16 NIV

Now when Jesus saw the crowds, he went up on a mountainside and sat down. His disciples came to him, and he began to teach them. He said: "Blessed are the poor in spirit, for theirs is the kingdom of heaven. Blessed are those who mourn, for they will be comforted. Blessed are the meek, for they will inherit the earth. Blessed are those who hunger and thirst for righteousness, for they will be filled. Blessed are the merciful, for they will be shown mercy. Blessed are the pure in heart, for they will see God. Blessed are the peacemakers, for they will be called children of God. Blessed are those who are persecuted because of righteousness, for theirs is the kingdom of heaven. Blessed are you when people insult you, persecute you and falsely say all kinds of evil against you because of me. Rejoice and be glad, because great is your reward in heaven, for in the same way they persecuted the prophets who were before you." MATTHEW 5:1–12 NIV

Jesus replied, "But even more blessed are all who hear the word of God and put it into practice." LUKE 11:28 NLT

Then Jesus led them to Bethany, and lifting his hands to heaven, he blessed them. While he was blessing them, he left them and was taken up to heaven. So they worshiped him and then returned to Jerusalem filled with great joy. And they spent all of their time in the Temple, praising God. LUKE 24:50–53 NLT

All praise to God, the Father of our Lord Jesus Christ, who has blessed us with every spiritual blessing in the heavenly realms because we are united with Christ. EPHESIANS 1:3 NLT

All praise to *God*,
the *Father* of our
Lord Jesus Christ . . .

Boldness

(willing to take risks; fearless)

In the day when I cried out, You answered me, *And* made me bold *with* strength in my soul. PSALM 138:3 NKJV

"'And then I'll stir up fresh hope in Israel—the dawn of deliverance!— and I'll give you, Ezekiel, bold and confident words to speak. And they'll realize that I am God.'" EZEKIEL 29:21 MSG

Now when they saw the boldness of Peter and John, and perceived that they were uneducated and untrained men, they marveled. And they realized that they had been with Jesus. ACTS 4:13 NKJV

"And now, O Lord, hear their threats, and give us, your servants, great boldness in preaching your word. Stretch out your hand with healing power; may miraculous signs and wonders be done through the name of your holy servant Jesus." After this prayer, the meeting place shook, and they were all filled with the Holy Spirit. Then they preached the word of God with boldness. ACTS 4:29–31 NLT

But the apostles stayed there a long time, preaching boldly about the grace of the Lord. And the Lord proved their message was true by giving them power to do miraculous signs and wonders. ACTS 14:3 NLT

Because of Christ and our faith in him, we can now come boldly and confidently into God's presence. EPHESIANS 3:12 NLT

And pray for me, too. Ask God to give me the right words so I can boldly explain God's mysterious plan that the Good News is for Jews and Gentiles alike. EPHESIANS 6:19 NLT

So let us come boldly to the throne of our gracious God. There we will receive his mercy, and we will find grace to help us when we need it most. HEBREWS 4:16 NLT

And so, dear brothers and sisters, we can boldly enter heaven's Most Holy Place because of the blood of Jesus. HEBREWS 10:19 NLT

You know how badly we had been treated at Philippi just before we came to you and how much we suffered there. Yet our God gave us the courage to declare his Good News to you boldly, in spite of great opposition. 1 THESSALONIANS 2:2 NLT

Love has been perfected among us in this: that we may have boldness in the day of judgment; because as He is, so are we in this world. 1 JOHN 4:17 NKJV

My purpose in writing is simply this: that you who believe in God's Son will know beyond the shadow of a doubt that you have eternal life, the reality and not the illusion. And how bold and free we then become in his presence, freely asking according to his will, sure that he's listening. And if we're confident that he's listening, we know that what we've asked for is as good as ours. 1 JOHN 5:13–15 MSG

Cleansing

(to make clean; to purify)

Cleanse me with hyssop, and I will be clean; wash me, and I will be whiter than snow. PSALM 51:7 NIV

Create in me a clean heart, O God, and renew a right spirit within me. PSALM 51:10 ESV

I will cleanse them from all the guilt of their sin against me, and I will forgive all the guilt of their sin and rebellion against me. JEREMIAH 33:8 ESV

I will sprinkle clean water on you, and you will be clean; I will cleanse you from all your impurities and from all your idols. I will give you a new heart and put a new spirit in you; I will remove from you your heart of stone and give you a heart of flesh. EZEKIEL 36:25–26 NIV

A man with leprosy came and knelt before him and said, "Lord, if you are willing, you can make me clean." Jesus reached out his hand and touched the man. "I am willing," he said. "Be clean!" Immediately he was cleansed of his leprosy. MATTHEW 8:2–3 NIV

For husbands, this means love your wives, just as Christ loved the church. He gave up his life for her to make her holy and clean, washed by the cleansing of God's word. He did this to present her to himself as a glorious church without a spot or wrinkle or any other blemish. Instead, she will be holy and without fault. EPHESIANS 5:25–27 NLT

God the Father knew you and chose you long ago, and his Spirit has made you holy. As a result, you have obeyed him and have been cleansed by the blood of Jesus Christ. May God give you more and more grace and peace. 1 PETER 1:2 NLT

Under the old system, the blood of goats and bulls and the ashes of a young cow could cleanse people's bodies from ceremonial impurity. Just think how much more the blood of Christ will purify our consciences from sinful deeds so that we can worship the living God. For by the power of the eternal Spirit, Christ offered himself to God as a perfect sacrifice for our sins. HEBREWS 9:13-14 NLT

But if we walk in the light, as he is in the light, we have fellowship with one another, and the blood of Jesus his Son cleanses us from all sin. If we say we have no sin, we deceive ourselves, and the truth is not in us. If we confess our sins, he is faithful and just to forgive us our sins and to cleanse us from all unrighteousness.
1 JOHN 1:7-9 ESV

If we *confess our sins,*
he is faithful and
just to *forgive . . .*

Comfort

*(to soothe pain or distress; to ease misery,
grief, or worry; to bring hope)*

Even when I walk through the darkest valley, I will not be afraid,
for you are close beside me. Your rod and your staff protect and
comfort me. **PSALM 23:4 NLT**

The LORD is near to the brokenhearted and saves the crushed in
spirit. **PSALM 34:18 ESV**

He heals the brokenhearted and binds up their wounds.
PSALM 147:3 NIV

"I, yes I, am the one who comforts you. So why are you afraid of mere
humans, who wither like the grass and disappear?" **ISAIAH 51:12 NLT**

Blessed are those who mourn, for they will be comforted.
MATTHEW 5:4 NIV

"I have told you these things, so that in me you may have peace. In
this world you will have trouble. But take heart! I have overcome
the world." **JOHN 16:33 NIV**

Keep your lives free from the love of money and be content with
what you have, because God has said, "Never will I leave you; never
will I forsake you." **HEBREWS 13:5 NIV**

Cast all your anxiety on him because he cares for you. **1 PETER 5:7 NIV**

Companionship

(to live, eat, or travel together; accompaniment)

Those who know your name trust in you, for you, O LORD, do not abandon those who search for you. PSALM 9:10 NLT

Even though I walk through the darkest valley, I will fear no evil, for you are with me; your rod and your staff, they comfort me. PSALM 23:4 NIV

For where two or three are gathered together in my name, there am I in the midst of them. MATTHEW 18:20 KJV

"Teach these new disciples to obey all the commands I have given you. And be sure of this: I am with you always, even to the end of the age." MATTHEW 28:20 NLT

Now it happened, as He was dining in *Levi's* house, that many tax collectors and sinners also sat together with Jesus and His disciples; for there were many, and they followed Him. MARK 2:15 NKJV

Jesus sent Peter and John ahead and said, "Go and prepare the Passover meal, so we can eat it together." . . . When the time came, Jesus and the apostles sat down together at the table. LUKE 22:8, 14 NLT

Now that same day two of them were going to a village called Emmaus, about seven miles from Jerusalem. They were talking with each other about everything that had happened. As they talked and discussed these things with each other, Jesus himself came up and walked along with them . . . LUKE 24:13–15 NIV

"For I am with you, and no one will attack and harm you, for many people in this city belong to me." ACTS 18:10 NLT

"For I am with you, and no one will attack and harm you, for many people in this city *belong to me."*

Compassion

(sorrow for the sufferings or trouble of others; sympathy that leads to an urge to help; pity)

But you, Lord, are a compassionate and gracious God, slow to anger, abounding in love and faithfulness. Turn to me and have mercy on me; show your strength in behalf of your servant; save me, because I serve you just as my mother did. **PSALM 86:15–16 NIV**

As a father shows compassion to his children, so the LORD shows compassion to those who fear him. **PSALM 103:13 ESV**

For if He causes grief, Then He will have compassion According to His abundant lovingkindness. **LAMENTATIONS 3:32 NASB**

Jesus saw the huge crowd as he stepped from the boat, and he had compassion on them and healed their sick. **MATTHEW 14:14 NLT**

Jesus called his disciples to him and said, "I have compassion for these people; they have already been with me three days and have nothing to eat. I do not want to send them away hungry, or they may collapse on the way." **MATTHEW 15:32 NIV**

Jesus saw the huge crowd as he stepped from the boat, and he had compassion on them because they were like sheep without a shepherd. So he began teaching them many things. **MARK 6:34 NLT**

When the Lord saw her, He felt compassion for her, and said to her, "Do not weep." **LUKE 7:13 NASB**

Brothers and sisters, as an example of patience in the face of suffering, take the prophets who spoke in the name of the Lord. As you know, we count as blessed those who have persevered. You have heard of Job's perseverance and have seen what the Lord finally brought about. The Lord is full of compassion and mercy.
JAMES 5:10–11 NIV

As you know, we count
as *blessed* those
who have persevered . . .
The *Lord* is full of
compassion and *mercy*.

⤫ Day 18 ⤫

Completion

(finish)

The LORD will fulfill his purpose for me; your steadfast love, O LORD, endures forever. Do not forsake the work of your hands.
PSALM 138:8 ESV

However, I consider my life worth nothing to me; my only aim is to finish the race and complete the task the Lord Jesus has given me—the task of testifying to the good news of God's grace.
ACTS 20:24 NIV

May you experience the love of Christ, though it is too great to understand fully. Then you will be made complete with all the fullness of life and power that comes from God. EPHESIANS 3:19 NLT

For in Christ lives all the fullness of God in a human body. So you also are complete through your union with Christ, who is the head over every ruler and authority. COLOSSIANS 2:9–10 NLT

I thank my God every time I remember you. In all my prayers for all of you, I always pray with joy because of your partnership in the gospel from the first day until now, being confident of this, that he who began a good work in you will carry it on to completion until the day of Christ Jesus. PHILIPPIANS 1:3–6 NIV

All Scripture *is* given by inspiration of God, and *is* profitable for doctrine, for reproof, for correction, for instruction in righteousness, that the man of God may be complete, thoroughly

∂⁄∂ *continued* ∂⁄∂

equipped for every good work. 2 TIMOTHY 3:16–17 NKJV

Do you see what this means—all these pioneers who blazed the way, all these veterans cheering us on? It means we'd better get on with it. Strip down, start running—and never quit! No extra spiritual fat, no parasitic sins. Keep your eyes on *Jesus*, who both began and finished this race we're in. Study how he did it. Because he never lost sight of where he was headed—that exhilarating finish in and with God—he could put up with anything along the way: Cross, shame, whatever. And now he's *there*, in the place of honor, right alongside God. When you find yourselves flagging in your faith, go over that story again, item by item, that long litany of hostility he plowed through. *That* will shoot adrenaline into your souls! HEBREWS 12:1–3 MSG

Keep your eyes on *Jesus*,
who both *began* and
finished this race we're in.

Contentment

*(happy with what one has/not desiring more;
satisfied; pleased)*

The LORD is my shepherd; I have all that I need. PSALM 23:1 NLT

I know that there is nothing better for people than to be happy and to do good while they live. That each of them may eat and drink, and find satisfaction in all their toil—this is the gift of God. ECCLESIASTES 3:12–13 NIV

I am not saying this because I am in need, for I have learned to be content whatever the circumstances. I know what it is to be in need, and I know what it is to have plenty. I have learned the secret of being content in any and every situation, whether well fed or hungry, whether living in plenty or in want. I can do all this through him who gives me strength. PHILIPPIANS 4:11–13 NIV

But godliness with contentment is great gain. For we brought nothing into the world, and we can take nothing out of it. But if we have food and clothing, we will be content with that. 1 TIMOTHY 6:6–8 NIV

Keep your life free from love of money, and be content with what you have, for he has said, "I will never leave you nor forsake you." HEBREWS 13:5 ESV

❧ Day 20 ❧

Correction

(to change from wrong to right; to point out errors)

People who accept discipline are on the pathway to life, but those who ignore correction will go astray. **PROVERBS 10:17 NLT**

To accept correction is wise, to reject it is stupid. **PROVERBS 12:1 CEV**

I know, LORD, that our lives are not our own. We are not able to plan our own course. So correct me, LORD, but please be gentle. Do not correct me in anger, for I would die. **JEREMIAH 10:23–24 NLT**

For our present troubles are small and won't last very long. Yet they produce for us a glory that vastly outweighs them and will last forever! **2 CORINTHIANS 4:17 NLT**

After all, you have not yet given your lives in your struggle against sin. And have you forgotten the encouraging words God spoke to you as his children? He said, "My child, don't make light of the LORD's discipline, and don't give up when he corrects you. For the LORD disciplines those he loves, and he punishes each one he accepts as his child." As you endure this divine discipline, remember that God is treating you as his own children. Who ever heard of a child who is never disciplined by its father? If God doesn't discipline you as he does all of his children, it means that you are illegitimate and are not really his children at all. Since we respected our earthly fathers who disciplined us, shouldn't we submit even more to the discipline of the Father of our spirits, and live forever? For our earthly fathers disciplined us for a few years, doing the best they knew how. But God's discipline is always good for us, so that we might share in his holiness. No discipline is enjoyable while it is happening—it's painful! But afterward there will be a peaceful harvest of right living for those who are trained in this way. HEBREWS 12:4–11 NLT

All Scripture *is* given by inspiration of God, and *is* profitable for doctrine, for reproof, for correction, for instruction in righteousness, that the man of God may be complete, thoroughly equipped for every good work. 2 TIMOTHY 3:16–17 NKJV

All *Scripture is* given by inspiration of God, and is profitable for doctrine, for reproof, for correction, *for instruction in righteousness…*

Courage

(bravery; willingness to face danger, difficulty, or the unknown)

"This is my command—be strong and courageous! Do not be afraid or discouraged. For the LORD your God is with you wherever you go." JOSHUA 1:9 NLT

David also said to Solomon his son, "Be strong and courageous, and do the work. Do not be afraid or discouraged, for the LORD God, my God, is with you. He will not fail you or forsake you until all the work for the service of the temple of the LORD is finished." 1 CHRONICLES 28:20 NIV

Wait on the LORD; Be of good courage, And He shall strengthen your heart; Wait, I say, on the LORD! PSALM 27:14 NKJV

When I asked for your help, you answered my prayer and gave me courage. PSALM 138:3 CEV

But Jesus immediately said to them: "Take courage! It is I. Don't be afraid." MATTHEW 14:27 NIV

Then the Son of Man will be seen, coming in a cloud with great power and glory. When all of this starts happening, stand up straight and be brave. You will soon be set free. LUKE 21:27–28 CEV

Be on guard. Stand firm in the faith. Be courageous. Be strong. And do everything with love. 1 CORINTHIANS 16:13–14 NLT

∽ continued ∽

Christ now gives us courage and confidence, so that we can come to God by faith. **EPHESIANS 3:12 CEV**

Be brave when you face your enemies. Your courage will show them that they are going to be destroyed, and it will show you that you will be saved. God will make all of this happen . . . **PHILIPPIANS 1:28 CEV**

For God hath not given us the spirit of fear; but of power, and of love, and of a sound mind. **2 TIMOTHY 1:7 KJV**

Christ gives me the courage to tell you what to do.
PHILEMON 1:8 CEV

My friends, the blood of Jesus gives us courage to enter the most holy place . . . **HEBREWS 10:19 CEV**

. . . the *blood of Jesus*
gives us courage to enter
the most *holy place.*

Deliverance

(to liberate; set free from danger)

"You will not have to fight this battle. Take up your positions; stand firm and see the deliverance the LORD will give you, Judah and Jerusalem. Do not be afraid; do not be discouraged. Go out to face them tomorrow, and the LORD will be with you."
2 CHRONICLES 20:17 NIV

The salvation of the righteous comes from the LORD; he is their stronghold in time of trouble. The LORD helps them and delivers them; he delivers them from the wicked and saves them, because they take refuge in him. **PSALM 37:39–40 NIV**

O give us help against the adversary, For deliverance by man is in vain. Through God we shall do valiantly, And it is He who will tread down our adversaries. **PSALM 60:11–12 NASB**

Though I walk in the midst of trouble, you preserve my life; you stretch out your hand against the wrath of my enemies, and your right hand delivers me. **PSALM 138:7 ESV**

But I will deliver you on that day, declares the LORD, and you shall not be given into the hand of the men of whom you are afraid.
JEREMIAH 39:17 ESV

This, then, is how you should pray: "Our Father in heaven, hallowed be your name, your kingdom come, your will be done, on earth as it is in heaven. Give us today our daily bread. And forgive us our debts, as we also have forgiven our debtors. And lead us not into temptation, but deliver us from the evil one." MATTHEW 6:9–13 NIV

What a wretched man I am! Who will rescue me from this body that is subject to death? Thanks be to God, who delivers me through Jesus Christ our Lord! So then, I myself in my mind am a slave to God's law, but in my sinful nature a slave to the law of sin. ROMANS 7:24–25 NIV

No temptation has overtaken you that is not common to man. God is faithful, and he will not let you be tempted beyond your ability, but with the temptation he will also provide the way of escape, that you may be able to endure it. 1 CORINTHIANS 10:13 ESV

He has delivered us from such a deadly peril, and he will deliver us again. On him we have set our hope that he will continue to deliver us . . . 2 CORINTHIANS 1:10 NIV

For I know that as you pray for me and the Spirit of Jesus Christ helps me, this will lead to my deliverance. PHILIPPIANS 1:19 NLT

Direction

(to show the way; to lead)

I will instruct you and teach you in the way you should go; I will counsel you with my loving eye on you. **PSALM 32:8 NIV**

And your ears shall hear a word behind you, saying, "This is the way, walk in it," when you turn to the right or when you turn to the left. **ISAIAH 30:21 ESV**

"You can enter God's Kingdom only through the narrow gate. The highway to hell is broad, and its gate is wide for the many who choose that way. But the gateway to life is very narrow and the road is difficult, and only a few ever find it." **MATTHEW 7:13-14 NLT**

After he has gathered his own flock, he walks ahead of them, and they follow him because they know his voice. **JOHN 10:4 NLT**

Thomas said to him, "Lord, we don't know where you are going, so how can we know the way?" Jesus answered, "I am the way and the truth and the life. No one comes to the Father except through me." **JOHN 14:5-6 NIV**

And now, just as you accepted Christ Jesus as your Lord, you must continue to follow him. **COLOSSIANS 2:6 NLT**

By faith Abraham, when called to go to a place he would later receive as his inheritance, obeyed and went, even though he did not know where he was going. **HEBREWS 11:8 NIV**

Discipline

(to punish; strict control to enforce obedience)

Think about it: Just as a parent disciplines a child, the LORD your God disciplines you for your own good. DEUTERONOMY 8:5 NLT

But if his descendants forsake my instructions and fail to obey my regulations, if they do not obey my decrees and fail to keep my commands, then I will punish their sin with the rod, and their disobedience with beating. But I will never stop loving him nor fail to keep my promise to him. PSALM 89:30–33 NLT

Blessed is the one you discipline, LORD, the one you teach from your law. PSALM 94:12 NIV

I know, O LORD, that your regulations are fair; you disciplined me because I needed it. PSALM 119:75 NLT

My child, don't reject the LORD's discipline, and don't be upset when he corrects you. For the LORD corrects those he loves, just as a father corrects a child in whom he delights. PROVERBS 3:11–12 NLT

People who accept discipline are on the pathway to life, but those who ignore correction will go astray. PROVERBS 10:17 NLT

"Blessed is the one whom God corrects; so do not despise the discipline of the Almighty." JOB 5:17 NIV

"For I am with you and will save you," says the LORD. "I will completely destroy the nations where I have scattered you, but I will not completely destroy you. I will discipline you, but with justice; I cannot let you go unpunished." JEREMIAH 30:11 NLT

"I am the true grapevine, and my Father is the gardener. He cuts off every branch of mine that doesn't produce fruit, and he prunes the branches that do bear fruit so they will produce even more. You have already been pruned and purified by the message I have given you. Remain in me, and I will remain in you. For a branch cannot produce fruit if it is severed from the vine, and you cannot be fruitful unless you remain in me. Yes, I am the vine; you are the branches. Those who remain in me, and I in them, will produce much fruit. For apart from me you can do nothing." JOHN 15:1–5 NLT

Yet when we are judged by the Lord, we are being disciplined so that we will not be condemned along with the world. 1 CORINTHIANS 11:32 NLT

Fathers, do not provoke your children to anger by the way you treat them. Rather, bring them up with the discipline and instruction that comes from the Lord. EPHESIANS 6:4 NLT

I correct and discipline everyone I love. So be diligent and turn from your indifference. REVELATION 3:19 NLT

Empathy

(ability to share another's emotions, thoughts, or feelings)

In all their suffering he also suffered, and he personally rescued them. In his love and mercy he redeemed them. He lifted them up and carried them through all the years. ISAIAH 63:9 NLT

When Mary reached the place where Jesus was and saw him, she fell at his feet and said, "Lord, if you had been here, my brother would not have died." When Jesus saw her weeping, and the Jews who had come along with her also weeping, he was deeply moved in spirit and troubled. "Where have you laid him?" he asked. "Come and see, Lord," they replied. Jesus wept. Then the Jews said, "See how he loved him!" JOHN 11:32–36 NLT

All praise to God, the Father of our Lord Jesus Christ. God is our merciful Father and the source of all comfort. He comforts us in all our troubles so that we can comfort others. When they are troubled, we will be able to give them the same comfort God has given us. 2 CORINTHIANS 1:3–4 NLT

Therefore, since we have a great high priest who has ascended into heaven, Jesus the Son of God, let us hold firmly to the faith we profess. For we do not have a high priest who is unable to empathize with our weaknesses, but we have one who has been tempted in every way, just as we are—yet he did not sin. Let us then approach God's throne of grace with confidence, so that we may receive mercy and find grace to help us in our time of need. HEBREWS 4:14–16 NIV

Encouragement

(to give support, confidence, or hope; to embolden)

But Jonathan went to see David, and God helped him encourage David. 1 SAMUEL 23:16 CEV

You, LORD, hear the desire of the afflicted; you encourage them, and you listen to their cry . . . PSALM 10:17 NIV

The humble will see their God at work and be glad. Let all who seek God's help be encouraged. PSALM 69:32 NLT

For I hold you by your right hand—I, the LORD your God. And I say to you, "Don't be afraid. I am here to help you." ISAIAH 41:13 NLT

The LORD God gives me the right words to encourage the weary. Each morning he awakens me eager to learn his teaching . . . ISAIAH 50:4 CEV

Then the church throughout Judea, Galilee and Samaria enjoyed a time of peace and was strengthened. Living in the fear of the Lord and encouraged by the Holy Spirit, it increased in numbers. ACTS 9:31 NIV

In his grace, God has given us different gifts for doing certain things well. So if God has given you the ability to prophesy, speak out with as much faith as God has given you. If your gift is serving others, serve them well. If you are a teacher, teach well. If your gift is to encourage others, be encouraging. If it is giving, give generously.

If God has given you leadership ability, take the responsibility seriously. And if you have a gift for showing kindness to others, do it gladly. **ROMANS 12:6–8 NLT**

Such things were written in the Scriptures long ago to teach us. And the Scriptures give us hope and encouragement as we wait patiently for God's promises to be fulfilled. May God, who gives this patience and encouragement, help you live in complete harmony with each other, as is fitting for followers of Christ Jesus. Then all of you can join together with one voice, giving praise and glory to God, the Father of our Lord Jesus Christ. **ROMANS 15:4–6 NLT**

But God, who encourages those who are discouraged, encouraged us by the arrival of Titus. **2 CORINTHIANS 7:6 NLT**

May our Lord Jesus Christ himself and God our Father, who loved us and by his grace gave us eternal encouragement and good hope, encourage your hearts and strengthen you in every good deed and word. **2 THESSALONIANS 2:16–17 NIV**

∽ *Day 27* ∽

Everything

(all things)

"You can pray for anything, and if you have faith, you will receive it." **MATTHEW 21:22 NLT**

Jesus looked at them intently and said, "Humanly speaking, it is impossible. But not with God. Everything is possible with God." **MARK 10:27 NLT**

And he is not served by human hands, as if he needed anything. Rather, he himself gives everyone life and breath and everything else. **ACTS 17:25 NIV**

He who did not spare his own Son, but gave him up for us all—how will he not also, along with him, graciously give us all things? **ROMANS 8:32 NIV**

But we know that there is only one God, the Father, who created everything, and we live for him. And there is only one Lord, Jesus Christ, through whom God made everything and through whom we have been given life. **1 CORINTHIANS 8:6 NLT**

The Son is the image of the invisible God, the firstborn over all creation. For in him all things were created: things in heaven and on earth, visible and invisible, whether thrones or powers or rulers or authorities; all things have been created through him and for him. He is before all things, and in him all things hold together. And he is the head of the body, the church; he is the beginning and the firstborn from among the dead, so that in everything he might have the supremacy. For God was pleased to have all his fullness dwell in him, and through him to reconcile to himself all things, whether things on earth or things in heaven, by making peace through his blood, shed on the cross. **COLOSSIANS 1:15–20 NIV**

And this same God who takes care of me will supply all your needs from his glorious riches, which have been given to us in Christ Jesus. **PHILIPPIANS 4:19 NLT**

By his divine power, God has given us everything we need for living a godly life. We have received all of this by coming to know him, the one who called us to himself by means of his marvelous glory and excellence. And because of his glory and excellence, he has given us great and precious promises. These are the promises that enable you to share his divine nature and escape the world's corruption caused by human desires. **2 PETER 1:3–4 NLT**

By his *divine power,*
God has given us
everything we need for
living a *godly life.*

☙ *Day 28* ❧

Exaltation

(to raise in status; to lift up)

And the LORD said to Joshua, "Today I will begin to exalt you in the eyes of all Israel, so they may know that I am with you as I was with Moses." JOSHUA 3:7 NIV

"The LORD sends poverty and wealth; he humbles and he exalts. He raises the poor from the dust and lifts the needy from the ash heap; he seats them with princes and has them inherit a throne of honor. For the foundations of the earth are the LORD's; on them he has set the world. He will guard the feet of his faithful servants, but the wicked will be silenced in the place of darkness. It is not by strength that one prevails; those who oppose the LORD will be broken. The Most High will thunder from heaven; the LORD will judge the ends of the earth. He will give strength to his king and exalt the horn of his anointed." 1 SAMUEL 2:7-10 NIV

"The LORD lives! Praise be to my Rock! Exalted be my God, the Rock, my Savior! He is the God who avenges me, who puts the nations under me, who sets me free from my enemies. You exalted me above my foes; from a violent man you rescued me. Therefore I will praise you, LORD, among the nations; I will sing the praises of your name." 2 SAMUEL 22:47-50 NIV

Now Solomon the son of David was strengthened in his kingdom, and the LORD his God *was* with him and exalted him exceedingly. 2 CHRONICLES 1:1 NKJV

continued

The LORD opens the eyes of the blind. The LORD lifts up those who are weighed down. The LORD loves the godly. **PSALM 146:8 NLT**

"For all those who exalt themselves will be humbled, and those who humble themselves will be exalted." **LUKE 18:14 NIV**

Humble yourselves therefore under the mighty hand of God, that he may exalt you in due time . . . **1 PETER 5:6 KJV**

Humble yourselves therefore under the mighty hand of *God*, that he may *exalt you* in due time...

Example

(model; precedent; something to be imitated)

One day Jesus was praying in a certain place. When he finished, one of his disciples said to him, "Lord, teach us to pray, just as John taught his disciples." He said to them, "When you pray, say: 'Father, hallowed be your name, your kingdom come. Give us each day our daily bread. Forgive us our sins, for we also forgive everyone who sins against us. And lead us not into temptation.'"
LUKE 11:1–4 NIV

Jesus gave them this answer: "Very truly I tell you, the Son can do nothing by himself; he can do only what he sees his Father doing, because whatever the Father does the Son also does." **JOHN 5:19 NIV**

After Jesus had washed his disciples' feet and had put his outer garment back on, he sat down again. Then he said: Do you understand what I have done? You call me your teacher and Lord, and you should, because that is who I am. And if your Lord and teacher has washed your feet, you should do the same for each other. I have set the example, and you should do for each other exactly what I have done for you. I tell you for certain that servants are not greater than their master, and messengers are not greater than the one who sent them. You know these things, and God will bless you, if you do them. **JOHN 13:12–17 CEV**

Follow my example, as I follow the example of Christ.
1 CORINTHIANS 11:1 NIV

Imitate God, therefore, in everything you do, because you are his dear children. Live a life filled with love, following the example of Christ. He loved us and offered himself as a sacrifice for us, a pleasing aroma to God. EPHESIANS 5:1–2 NLT

For God called you to do good, even if it means suffering, just as Christ suffered for you. He is your example, and you must follow in his steps. He never sinned, nor ever deceived anyone. He did not retaliate when he was insulted, nor threaten revenge when he suffered. He left his case in the hands of God, who always judges fairly. He personally carried our sins in his body on the cross so that we can be dead to sin and live for what is right. By his wounds you are healed. Once you were like sheep who wandered away. But now you have turned to your Shepherd, the Guardian of your souls. 1 PETER 2:21–25 NLT

Now follow the example of the correct teaching I gave you, and let the faith and love of Christ Jesus be your model. 2 TIMOTHY 1:13 CEV

If we say we are his, we must follow the example of Christ. 1 JOHN 2:6 CEV

Faith

(unquestioning belief that does not require proof or evidence; complete trust)

"You don't have enough faith," Jesus told them. "I tell you the truth, if you had faith even as small as a mustard seed, you could say to this mountain, 'Move from here to there,' and it would move. Nothing would be impossible." **MATTHEW 17:20 NLT**

Jesus replied, "Why do you say 'if you can'? Anything is possible for someone who has faith!" Right away the boy's father shouted, "I do have faith! Please help me to have even more." **MARK 9:23–24 CEV**

The apostles said to the Lord, "Increase our faith!" He replied, "If you have faith as small as a mustard seed, you can say to this mulberry tree, 'Be uprooted and planted in the sea,' and it will obey you." **LUKE 17:5-6 NIV**

So faith *comes* from hearing, and hearing by the word of Christ. **ROMANS 10:17 NASB**

But the fruit of the Spirit is love, joy, peace, longsuffering, gentleness, goodness, faith, Meekness, temperance: against such there is no law. **GALATIANS 5:22–23 KJV**

For it is by grace you have been saved, through faith—and this is not from yourselves, it is the gift of God— not by works, so that no one can boast. **EPHESIANS 2:8-9 NIV**

Now faith is confidence in what we hope for and assurance about what we do not see. This is what the ancients were commended for. By faith we understand that the universe was formed at God's command, so that what is seen was not made out of what was visible. By faith Abel brought God a better offering than Cain did. By faith he was commended as righteous, when God spoke well of his offerings. And by faith Abel still speaks, even though he is dead. By faith Enoch was taken from this life, so that he did not experience death: "He could not be found, because God had taken him away." For before he was taken, he was commended as one who pleased God. And without faith it is impossible to please God, because anyone who comes to him must believe that he exists and that he rewards those who earnestly seek him. **HEBREWS 11:1–6 NIV**

Therefore, since we have so great a cloud of witnesses surrounding us, let us also lay aside every encumbrance and the sin which so easily entangles us, and let us run with endurance the race that is set before us, fixing our eyes on Jesus, the author and perfecter of faith, who for the joy set before Him endured the cross, despising the shame, and has sat down at the right hand of the throne of God. **HEBREWS 12:1–2 NASB**

Listen, my beloved brothers, has not God chosen those who are poor in the world to be rich in faith and heirs of the kingdom, which he has promised to those who love him? **JAMES 2:5 ESV**

Faithfulness

(loyal; reliable)

Know therefore that the Lord your God is God; he is the faithful God, keeping his covenant of love to a thousand generations of those who love him and keep his commandments.
DEUTERONOMY 7:9 NIV

So the Word became human and made his home among us. He was full of unfailing love and faithfulness. And we have seen his glory, the glory of the Father's one and only Son. John testified about him when he shouted to the crowds, "This is the one I was talking about when I said, 'Someone is coming after me who is far greater than I am, for he existed long before me.'" From his abundance we have all received one gracious blessing after another. For the law was given through Moses, but God's unfailing love and faithfulness came through Jesus Christ. **JOHN 1:14–17 NLT**

God is faithful, who has called you into fellowship with his Son, Jesus Christ our Lord. **1 CORINTHIANS 1:9 NIV**

But the Holy Spirit produces this kind of fruit in our lives: love, joy, peace, patience, kindness, goodness, faithfulness, gentleness, and self-control. There is no law against these things!
GALATIANS 5:22–23 NLT

Favor

*(special privilege; indulgence;
undeserved partiality; kindness)*

For it is You who blesses the righteous man, O LORD, You surround him with favor as with a shield. **PSALM 5:12 NASB**

For his anger lasts only a moment, but his favor lasts a lifetime! Weeping may last through the night, but joy comes with the morning. **PSALM 30:5 NLT**

For the LORD God is a sun and shield; the LORD bestows favor and honor; no good thing does he withhold from those whose walk is blameless. **PSALM 84:11 NIV**

Toward the scorners he is scornful, but to the humble he gives favor. **PROVERBS 3:34 ESV**

Good people obtain favor from the LORD, but he condemns those who devise wicked schemes. **PROVERBS 12:2 NIV**

When people's lives please the LORD, even their enemies are at peace with them. **PROVERBS 16:7 NLT**

"The Lord has done this for me," she said. "In these days he has shown his favor and taken away my disgrace among the people." **LUKE 1:25 NIV**

And having come in, the angel said to her, "Rejoice, highly favored *one*, the LORD *is* with you; blessed *are* you among women!" But when she saw *him*, she was troubled at his saying, and considered what manner of greeting this was. Then the angel said to her, "Do not be afraid, Mary, for you have found favor with God." LUKE 1:28–30 NKJV

"Glory to God in the highest heaven, and on earth peace to those on whom his favor rests." LUKE 2:14 NIV

"The Spirit of the Lord is on me, because he has anointed me to proclaim good news to the poor. He has sent me to proclaim freedom for the prisoners and recovery of sight for the blind, to set the oppressed free, to proclaim the year of the Lord's favor." LUKE 4:18–19 NIV

"...to set the *oppressed* free, to proclaim the year of the *Lord's favor*."

Fellowship

(mutual sharing of experience; brotherhood)

Later, Levi invited Jesus and his disciples to his home as dinner guests, along with many tax collectors and other disreputable sinners. (There were many people of this kind among Jesus' followers.) But when the teachers of religious law who were Pharisees saw him eating with tax collectors and other sinners, they asked his disciples, "Why does he eat with such scum?" When Jesus heard this, he told them, "Healthy people don't need a doctor—sick people do. I have come to call not those who think they are righteous, but those who know they are sinners." **MARK 2:15–17 NLT**

"King David said this about him: 'I see that the Lord is always with me. I will not be shaken, for he is right beside me. No wonder my heart is glad, and my tongue shouts his praises! My body rests in hope. For you will not leave my soul among the dead or allow your Holy One to rot in the grave. You have shown me the way of life, and you will fill me with the joy of your presence.'" **ACTS 2:25–28 NLT**

And we know that the Son of God has come, and he has given us understanding so that we can know the true God. And now we live in fellowship with the true God because we live in fellowship with his Son, Jesus Christ. He is the only true God, and he is eternal life. **1 JOHN 5:20 NLT**

"Look! I stand at the door and knock. If you hear my voice and open the door, I will come in, and we will share a meal together as friends." **REVELATION 3:20 NLT**

continued

Then I saw "a new heaven and a new earth," for the first heaven and the first earth had passed away, and there was no longer any sea. I saw the Holy City, the new Jerusalem, coming down out of heaven from God, prepared as a bride beautifully dressed for her husband. And I heard a loud voice from the throne saying, "Look! God's dwelling place is now among the people, and he will dwell with them. They will be his people, and God himself will be with them and be their God. 'He will wipe every tear from their eyes. There will be no more death' or mourning or crying or pain, for the old order of things has passed away." REVELATION 21:1–4 NIV

"'There will be *no more death*' or *mourning* or crying or pain, for the *old order of things* has passed away."

Forgiveness

*(to give up resentment or the desire to punish;
to stop being angry)*

They refused to listen and failed to remember the miracles you performed among them. They became stiff-necked and in their rebellion appointed a leader in order to return to their slavery. But you are a forgiving God, gracious and compassionate, slow to anger and abounding in love. Therefore you did not desert them . . . NEHEMIAH 9:17 NIV

"So I will prove to you that the Son of Man has the authority on earth to forgive sins." Then Jesus turned to the paralyzed man and said, "Stand up, pick up your mat, and go home!" And the man jumped up and went home! MATTHEW 9:6–7 NLT

This is my blood of the covenant, which is poured out for many for the forgiveness of sins. MATTHEW 26:28 NIV

Seeing their faith, Jesus said to the paralyzed man, "My child, your sins are forgiven." MARK 2:5 NLT

"And when you stand praying, if you hold anything against anyone, forgive them, so that your Father in heaven may forgive you your sins." MARK 11:25 NIV

The very next day John saw Jesus coming toward him and yelled out, "Here he is, God's Passover Lamb! He forgives the sins of the world! This is the man I've been talking about, 'the One who comes after me but is really ahead of me.' I knew nothing about who he was—only this: that my task has been to get Israel ready to recognize him as the God-Revealer. That is why I came here baptizing with water, giving you a good bath and scrubbing sins from your life so you can get a fresh start with God." JOHN 1:29–31 MSG

"He is the one all the prophets testified about, saying that everyone who believes in him will have their sins forgiven through his name." ACTS 10:43 NLT

"Brothers, listen! We are here to proclaim that through this man Jesus there is forgiveness for your sins." ACTS 13:38 NLT

Be kind and compassionate to one another, forgiving each other, just as in Christ God forgave you. EPHESIANS 4:32 NIV

Therefore, as God's chosen people, holy and dearly loved, clothe yourselves with compassion, kindness, humility, gentleness and patience. Bear with each other and forgive one another if any of you has a grievance against someone. Forgive as the Lord forgave you. And over all these virtues put on love, which binds them all together in perfect unity. COLOSSIANS 3:12–14 NIV

Freedom

(liberation)

God places the lonely in families; he sets the prisoners free and gives them joy. But he makes the rebellious live in a sun-scorched land. PSALM 68:6 NLT

"The Spirit of the Lord is on me, because he has anointed me to proclaim good news to the poor. He has sent me to proclaim freedom for the prisoners and recovery of sight for the blind, to set the oppressed free." LUKE 4:18 NIV

To the Jews who had believed him, Jesus said, "If you hold to my teaching, you are really my disciples. Then you will know the truth, and the truth will set you free." They answered him, "We are Abraham's descendants and have never been slaves of anyone. How can you say that we shall be set free?" Jesus replied, "Very truly I tell you, everyone who sins is a slave to sin. Now a slave has no permanent place in the family, but a son belongs to it forever. So if the Son sets you free, you will be free indeed." JOHN 8:31–36 NIV

Sin is no longer your master, for you no longer live under the requirements of the law. Instead, you live under the freedom of God's grace. ROMANS 6:14 NLT

Therefore, there is now no condemnation for those who are in Christ Jesus, because through Christ Jesus the law of the Spirit who gives life has set you free from the law of sin and death. For what the law was powerless to do because it was weakened by the flesh, God did by sending his own Son in the likeness of sinful flesh to be a sin offering. And so he condemned sin in the flesh, in order that the righteous requirement of the law might be fully met in us, who do not live according to the flesh but according to the Spirit. ROMANS 8:1–4 NIV

For the Lord is the Spirit, and wherever the Spirit of the Lord is, there is freedom. 2 CORINTHIANS 3:17 NLT

It is for freedom that Christ has set us free. Stand firm, then, and do not let yourselves be burdened again by a yoke of slavery . . . You, my brothers and sisters, were called to be free. But do not use your freedom to indulge the flesh; rather, serve one another humbly in love. For the entire law is fulfilled in keeping this one command: "Love your neighbor as yourself." GALATIANS 5:1, 13–14 NIV

You, my *brothers*
and *sisters*, were called
to be free.

Fulfillment

(to fill the requirements of; to carry out a promise)

For the LORD God is our sun and our shield. He gives us grace and glory. The LORD will withhold no good thing from those who do what is right. PSALM 84:11 NLT

Let them give thanks to the LORD for his unfailing love and his wonderful deeds for mankind, for he satisfies the thirsty and fills the hungry with good things. PSALM 107:8–9 NIV

The Lord is near to all who call on him, to all who call on him in truth. He fulfills the desires of those who fear him; he hears their cry and saves them. PSALM 145:18–19 NIV

Blessed are those who hunger and thirst for righteousness, for they will be filled . . . "Do not think that I have come to abolish the Law or the Prophets; I have not come to abolish them but to fulfill them." MATTHEW 5:6, 17 NIV

As the Father has loved me, so have I loved you. Abide in my love. If you keep my commandments, you will abide in my love, just as I have kept my Father's commandments and abide in his love. These things I have spoken to you, that my joy may be in you, and that your joy may be full. JOHN 15:9–11 ESV

In him we have redemption through his blood, the forgiveness of sins, in accordance with the riches of God's grace that he lavished on us. With all wisdom and understanding, he made known to us the mystery of his will according to his good pleasure, which he purposed in Christ, to be put into effect when the times reach their fulfillment—to bring unity to all things in heaven and on earth under Christ. EPHESIANS 1:7–10 NIV

And the church is his body; it is made full and complete by Christ, who fills all things everywhere with himself. EPHESIANS 1:23 NLT

Let us hold tightly without wavering to the hope we affirm, for God can be trusted to keep his promise . . . Patient endurance is what you need now, so that you will continue to do God's will. Then you will receive all that he has promised. HEBREWS 10:23, 36 NLT

Let us *hold tightly* without wavering to the hope we affirm, for *God can be trusted* to keep his promise…

Gentleness

(not violent, harsh, or rough)

The LORD said, "Go out and stand on the mountain in the presence of the LORD, for the LORD is about to pass by." Then a great and powerful wind tore the mountains apart and shattered the rocks before the LORD, but the LORD was not in the wind. After the wind there was an earthquake, but the LORD was not in the earthquake. After the earthquake came a fire, but the LORD was not in the fire. And after the fire came a gentle whisper. When Elijah heard it, he pulled his cloak over his face and went out and stood at the mouth of the cave. Then a voice said to him, "What are you doing here, Elijah?" 1 KINGS 19:11–13 NIV

But the fruit of the Spirit is love, joy, peace, forbearance, kindness, goodness, faithfulness, gentleness and self-control. Against such things there is no law. GALATIANS 5:22–23 NIV

I, therefore, the prisoner of the Lord, beseech you to walk worthy of the calling with which you were called, with all lowliness and gentleness, with longsuffering, bearing with one another in love, endeavoring to keep the unity of the Spirit in the bond of peace. EPHESIANS 4:1–3 NKJV

But you, O man of God, flee these things and pursue righteousness, godliness, faith, love, patience, gentleness. Fight the good fight of faith, lay hold on eternal life, to which you were also called and have confessed the good confession in the presence of many witnesses. 1 TIMOTHY 6:11–12 NKJV

But the wisdom that is from above is first pure, then peaceable, gentle, willing to yield, full of mercy and good fruits, without partiality and without hypocrisy. JAMES 3:17 NKJV

Do not let your adornment be *merely* outward—arranging the hair, wearing gold, or putting on *fine* apparel—rather *let it* be the hidden person of the heart, with the incorruptible *beauty* of a gentle and quiet spirit, which is very precious in the sight of God. 1 PETER 3:3–4 NKJV

Timothy, you belong to God, so keep away from all these evil things. Try your best to please God and to be like him. Be faithful, loving, dependable, and gentle. 1 TIMOTHY 6:11 CEV

Take my yoke upon you. Let me teach you, because I am humble and gentle at heart, and you will find rest for your souls. MATTHEW 11:29 NLT

Let me teach you,
because I am humble
and *gentle at heart…*

Glory

(radiant beauty or splendor; heaven)

He will give eternal life to those who keep on doing good, seeking after the glory and honor and immortality that God offers.
ROMANS 2:7 NLT

But all who do right will be rewarded with glory, honor, and peace, whether they are Jews or Gentiles. ROMANS 2:10 CEV

Therefore, since we have been made right in God's sight by faith, we have peace with God because of what Jesus Christ our Lord has done for us. Because of our faith, Christ has brought us into this place of undeserved privilege where we now stand, and we confidently and joyfully look forward to sharing God's glory.
ROMANS 5:1–2 NLT

And since we are his children, we are his heirs. In fact, together with Christ we are heirs of God's glory. But if we are to share his glory, we must also share his suffering. Yet what we suffer now is nothing compared to the glory he will reveal to us later. ROMANS 8:17–18 NLT

The old way, with laws etched in stone, led to death, though it began with such glory that the people of Israel could not bear to look at Moses' face. For his face shone with the glory of God, even though the brightness was already fading away. Shouldn't we expect far greater glory under the new way, now that the Holy Spirit is giving life? If the old way, which brings condemnation, was glorious, how much more glorious is the new way, which makes us right with

God! In fact, that first glory was not glorious at all compared with the overwhelming glory of the new way. So if the old way, which has been replaced, was glorious, how much more glorious is the new, which remains forever! 2 CORINTHIANS 3:7–11 NLT

But we all, with unveiled face, beholding as in a mirror the glory of the Lord, are being transformed into the same image from glory to glory, just as by the Spirit of the Lord.
2 CORINTHIANS 3:18 NKJV

For God wanted them to know that the riches and glory of Christ are for you Gentiles, too. And this is the secret: Christ lives in you. This gives you assurance of sharing his glory. COLOSSIANS 1:27 NLT

God, for whom and through whom everything was made, chose to bring many children into glory. And it was only right that he should make Jesus, through his suffering, a perfect leader, fit to bring them into their salvation. HEBREWS 2:10 NLT

In his kindness God called you to share in his eternal glory by means of Christ Jesus. So after you have suffered a little while, he will restore, support, and strengthen you, and he will place you on a firm foundation. 1 PETER 5:10 NLT

Good News

(gospel)

Later on, after John was arrested, Jesus went into Galilee, where he preached God's Good News. "The time promised by God has come at last!" he announced. "The Kingdom of God is near! Repent of your sins and believe the Good News!" MARK 1:14–15 NLT

And then he told them, "Go into all the world and preach the Good News to everyone. Anyone who believes and is baptized will be saved. But anyone who refuses to believe will be condemned." MARK 16:15–16 NLT

Early the next morning Jesus went out to an isolated place. The crowds searched everywhere for him, and when they finally found him, they begged him not to leave them. But he replied, "I must preach the Good News of the Kingdom of God in other towns, too, because that is why I was sent." So he continued to travel around, preaching in synagogues throughout Judea. LUKE 4:42–44 NLT

For I am not ashamed of this Good News about Christ. It is the power of God at work, saving everyone who believes—the Jew first and also the Gentile. This Good News tells us how God makes us right in his sight. This is accomplished from start to finish by faith. As the Scriptures say, "It is through faith that a righteous person has life." ROMANS 1:16–17 NLT

This same Good News that came to you is going out all over the world. It is bearing fruit everywhere by changing lives, just as it changed your lives from the day you first heard and understood the truth about God's wonderful grace. COLOSSIANS 1:6 NLT

And now he has made all of this plain to us by the appearing of Christ Jesus, our Savior. He broke the power of death and illuminated the way to life and immortality through the Good News. 2 TIMOTHY 1:10 NLT

This is love: not that we loved God, but that he loved us and sent his Son as an atoning sacrifice for our sins. 1 JOHN 4:10 NIV

And this is what God has testified: He has given us eternal life, and this life is in his Son. Whoever has the Son has life; whoever does not have God's Son does not have life. 1 JOHN 5:11–12 NLT

...He has given us *eternal life*, and this life is in *his Son*.

Goodness

(excellence)

They shall come and sing aloud on the height of Zion, and they shall be radiant over the goodness of the LORD, over the grain, the wine, and the oil, and over the young of the flock and the herd; their life shall be like a watered garden, and they shall languish no more. JEREMIAH 31:12 ESV

"Ask, and it will be given to you; seek, and you will find; knock, and it will be opened to you. For everyone who asks receives, and he who seeks finds, and to him who knocks it will be opened. Or what man is there among you who, when his son asks for a loaf, will give him a stone? Or if he asks for a fish, he will not give him a snake, will he? If you then, being evil, know how to give good gifts to your children, how much more will your Father who is in heaven give what is good to those who ask Him!" MATTHEW 7:7–11 NASB

"In the past he permitted all the nations to go their own ways, but he never left them without evidence of himself and his goodness. For instance, he sends you rain and good crops and gives you food and joyful hearts." ACTS 14:16–17 NLT

"For last night an angel of the God to whom I belong and whom I serve stood beside me, and he said, 'Don't be afraid, Paul, for you will surely stand trial before Caesar! What's more, God in his goodness has granted safety to everyone sailing with you.' So take courage! For I believe God. It will be just as he said." ACTS 27:23–25 NLT

Or do you despise the riches of His goodness, forbearance, and longsuffering, not knowing that the goodness of God leads you to repentance? ROMANS 2:4 NKJV

For you were once darkness, but now you are light in the Lord. Live as children of light (for the fruit of the light consists in all goodness, righteousness and truth) and find out what pleases the Lord. EPHESIANS 5:8–10 NIV

But you are not like that, for you are a chosen people. You are royal priests, a holy nation, God's very own possession. As a result, you can show others the goodness of God, for he called you out of the darkness into his wonderful light. 1 PETER 2:9 NLT

…you can show others the *goodness of God*, for he called you out of the darkness into *his wonderful light.*

Grace

*(unmerited love and favor of God toward humans; a
special virtue, gift, or help given by God)*

The Word became flesh and made his dwelling among us. We have
seen his glory, the glory of the one and only Son, who came from
the Father, full of grace and truth. (John testified concerning him.
He cried out, saying, "This is the one I spoke about when I said,
'He who comes after me has surpassed me because he was before
me.'") Out of his fullness we have all received grace in place of
grace already given. For the law was given through Moses; grace
and truth came through Jesus Christ. No one has ever seen God,
but the one and only Son, who is himself God and is in closest
relationship with the Father, has made him known. JOHN 1:14–18 NIV

Through him we received grace and apostleship to call all the
Gentiles to the obedience that comes from faith for his name's
sake. ROMANS 1:5 NIV

Moreover the law entered, that the offence might abound. But
where sin abounded, grace did much more abound: That as sin
hath reigned unto death, even so might grace reign through
righteousness unto eternal life by Jesus Christ our Lord.
ROMANS 5:20–21 KJV

I thank my God always on your behalf, for the grace of God which
is given you by Jesus Christ . . . 1 CORINTHIANS 1:4 KJV

But he said to me, "My grace is sufficient for you, for my power
is made perfect in weakness." Therefore I will boast all the more

gladly about my weaknesses, so that Christ's power may rest on me. 2 CORINTHIANS 12:9 NIV

In him we have redemption through his blood, the forgiveness of sins, in accordance with the riches of God's grace that he lavished on us. EPHESIANS 1:7–8 NIV

But because of his great love for us, God, who is rich in mercy, made us alive with Christ even when we were dead in transgressions—it is by grace you have been saved. And God raised us up with Christ and seated us with him in the heavenly realms in Christ Jesus, in order that in the coming ages he might show the incomparable riches of his grace, expressed in his kindness to us in Christ Jesus. For it is by grace you have been saved, through faith—and this is not from yourselves, it is the gift of God—not by works, so that no one can boast. For we are God's handiwork, created in Christ Jesus to do good works, which God prepared in advance for us to do. EPHESIANS 2:4–10 NIV

Each of you should use whatever gift you have received to serve others, as faithful stewards of God's grace in its various forms. 1 PETER 4:10 NIV

As God's co-workers we urge you not to receive God's grace in vain. 2 CORINTHIANS 6:1 NIV

Growth

(maturity; development)

Don't become so well-adjusted to your culture that you fit into it without even thinking. Instead, fix your attention on God. You'll be changed from the inside out. Readily recognize what he wants from you, and quickly respond to it. Unlike the culture around you, always dragging you down to its level of immaturity, God brings the best out of you, develops well-formed maturity in you.
ROMANS 12:2 MSG

When one of you says, "I am a follower of Paul," and another says, "I follow Apollos," aren't you acting just like people of the world? After all, who is Apollos? Who is Paul? We are only God's servants through whom you believed the Good News. Each of us did the work the Lord gave us. I planted the seed in your hearts, and Apollos watered it, but it was God who made it grow. It's not important who does the planting, or who does the watering. What's important is that God makes the seed grow. The one who plants and the one who waters work together with the same purpose. And both will be rewarded for their own hard work. For we are both God's workers. And you are God's field. You are God's building.
1 CORINTHIANS 3:4–9 NLT

Like newborn babies, you must crave pure spiritual milk so that you will grow into a full experience of salvation. Cry out for this nourishment, now that you have had a taste of the Lord's kindness.
1 PETER 2:2–3 NLT

continued

In view of all this, make every effort to respond to God's promises. Supplement your faith with a generous provision of moral excellence, and moral excellence with knowledge, and knowledge with self-control, and self-control with patient endurance, and patient endurance with godliness, and godliness with brotherly affection, and brotherly affection with love for everyone. The more you grow like this, the more productive and useful you will be in your knowledge of our Lord Jesus Christ. But those who fail to develop in this way are shortsighted or blind, forgetting that they have been cleansed from their old sins. 2 PETER 1:5–9 NLT

The more you *grow* like this, the more *productive and useful* you will be in your knowledge of our *Lord Jesus Christ.*

Guidance

(to point out the way; to keep straight)

He lets me rest in green meadows; he leads me beside peaceful streams. He renews my strength. He guides me along right paths, bringing honor to his name. PSALM 23:2–3 NLT

For this God is our God for ever and ever: he will be our guide even unto death. PSALM 48:14 KJV

Trust in the LORD with all your heart and lean not on your own understanding; in all your ways submit to him, and he will make your paths straight. PROVERBS 3:5–6 NIV

They will neither hunger nor thirst, nor will the desert heat or the sun beat down on them. He who has compassion on them will guide them and lead them beside springs of water. ISAIAH 49:10 NIV

"And you, my child, will be called a prophet of the Most High; for you will go on before the Lord to prepare the way for him, to give his people the knowledge of salvation through the forgiveness of their sins, because of the tender mercy of our God, by which the rising sun will come to us from heaven to shine on those living in darkness and in the shadow of death, to guide our feet into the path of peace." LUKE 1:76–79 NIV

When the Spirit of truth comes, he will guide you into all truth. He will not speak on his own but will tell you what he has heard. He will tell you about the future. JOHN 16:13 NLT

We can be proud of our clear conscience. We have always lived honestly and sincerely, especially when we were with you. And we were guided by God's wonderful kindness instead of by the wisdom of this world. 2 CORINTHIANS 1:12 CEV

So I say, let the Holy Spirit guide your lives. Then you won't be doing what your sinful nature craves. GALATIANS 5:16 NLT

Let love be your guide. Christ loved us and offered his life for us as a sacrifice that pleases God. EPHESIANS 5:2 CEV

I pray that the Lord will guide you to be as loving as God and as patient as Christ. 2 THESSALONIANS 3:5 CEV

…the Lord will *guide* you
to be *as loving as God* and
as *patient as Christ.*

∞ *Day 44* ∞

Happiness

(pleasure; bright spirits)

May the LORD bless his people with peace and happiness and let them celebrate. PSALM 64:10 CEV

For a sun and a shield [is] Jehovah God, Grace and honour doth Jehovah give. He withholdeth not good To those walking in uprightness. Jehovah of Hosts! O the happiness of a man trusting in Thee. PSALM 84:11-12 YLT

Give me happiness, O Lord, for I give myself to you. PSALM 86:4 NLT

To the person who pleases him, God gives wisdom, knowledge and happiness, but to the sinner he gives the task of gathering and storing up wealth to hand it over to the one who pleases God. This too is meaningless, a chasing after the wind. ECCLESIASTES 2:26 NIV

I know the best thing we can do is to always enjoy life, because God's gift to us is the happiness we get from our food and drink and from the work we do. Everything God has done will last forever; nothing he does can ever be changed. God has done all this, so that we will worship him. ECCLESIASTES 3:12-14 CEV

The people the LORD has rescued will come back singing as they enter Zion. Happiness will be a crown they will always wear. They will celebrate and shout because all sorrows and worries will be gone far away. ISAIAH 35:10 CEV

◈ continued ◈

I create light and darkness, happiness and sorrow. I, the LORD, do all of this. ISAIAH 45:7 CEV

Young women and young men, together with the elderly, will celebrate and dance, because I will comfort them and turn their sorrow into happiness. JEREMIAH 31:13 CEV

Happy those hungering now—because ye shall be filled. Happy those weeping now--because ye shall laugh. LUKE 6:21 YLT

God's kingdom isn't about eating and drinking. It is about pleasing God, about living in peace, and about true happiness. All this comes from the Holy Spirit. ROMANS 14:17 CEV

I pray that God, who gives hope, will bless you with complete happiness and peace because of your faith. And may the power of the Holy Spirit fill you with hope. ROMANS 15:13 CEV

...God, who gives
hope, will bless
you with complete
happiness and peace...

Healing

(to restore to health; to make well)

Surely he took up our pain and bore our suffering, yet we considered him punished by God, stricken by him, and afflicted. But he was pierced for our transgressions, he was crushed for our iniquities; the punishment that brought us peace was on him, and by his wounds we are healed. ISAIAH 53:4–5 NIV

Jesus went throughout Galilee, teaching in their synagogues, proclaiming the good news of the kingdom, and healing every disease and sickness among the people. News about him spread all over Syria, and people brought to him all who were ill with various diseases, those suffering severe pain, the demon-possessed, those having seizures, and the paralyzed; and he healed them.
MATTHEW 4:23–24 NIV

When Jesus returned to Capernaum, a Roman officer came and pleaded with him, "Lord, my young servant lies in bed, paralyzed and in terrible pain." Jesus said, "I will come and heal him." But the officer said, "Lord, I am not worthy to have you come into my home. Just say the word from where you are, and my servant will be healed. I know this because I am under the authority of my superior officers, and I have authority over my soldiers. I only need to say, 'Go,' and they go, or 'Come,' and they come. And if I say to my slaves, 'Do this,' they do it." When Jesus heard this, he was amazed. Turning to those who were following him, he said, "I tell you the truth, I haven't seen faith like this in all Israel!" . . . Then Jesus said to the Roman officer, "Go back home. Because you believed, it has happened." And the young servant was healed that same hour. MATTHEW 8:5–10, 13 NLT

When Jesus came into Peter's house, he saw Peter's mother-in-law lying in bed with a fever. He touched her hand and the fever left her, and she got up and began to wait on him. When evening came, many who were demon-possessed were brought to him, and he drove out the spirits with a word and healed all the sick. This was to fulfill what was spoken through the prophet Isaiah: "He took up our infirmities and bore our diseases." MATTHEW 8:14–17 NIV

Just then a woman who had suffered for twelve years with constant bleeding came up behind him. She touched the fringe of his robe, for she thought, "If I can just touch his robe, I will be healed." Jesus turned around, and when he saw her he said, "Daughter, be encouraged! Your faith has made you well." And the woman was healed at that moment. MATTHEW 9:20–22 NLT

Great crowds came to him, bringing the lame, the blind, the crippled, the mute and many others, and laid them at his feet; and he healed them. The people were amazed when they saw the mute speaking, the crippled made well, the lame walking and the blind seeing. And they praised the God of Israel. MATTHEW 15:30–31 NIV

Everyone tried to touch him, because healing power went out from him, and he healed everyone. LUKE 6:19 NLT

Holy Spirit

(the third person of the Trinity)

And I will ask the Father, and he will give you another Advocate, who will never leave you. He is the Holy Spirit, who leads into all truth. The world cannot receive him, because it isn't looking for him and doesn't recognize him. But you know him, because he lives with you now and later will be in you. JOHN 14:16–17 NLT

But I tell you that I am going to do what is best for you. That is why I am going away. The Holy Spirit cannot come to help you until I leave. But after I am gone, I will send the Spirit to you. JOHN 16:7 CEV

Then he breathed on them and said, "Receive the Holy Spirit." JOHN 20:22 NLT

Jesus was taken up to sit at the right side of God, and he was given the Holy Spirit, just as the Father had promised. Jesus is also the one who has given the Spirit to us, and that is what you are now seeing and hearing. ACTS 2:33 CEV

Peter replied, "Each of you must repent of your sins and turn to God, and be baptized in the name of Jesus Christ for the forgiveness of your sins. Then you will receive the gift of the Holy Spirit. This promise is to you, and to your children, and even to the Gentiles—all who have been called by the Lord our God." ACTS 2:38–39 NLT

Now hope does not disappoint, because the love of God has been

poured out in our hearts by the Holy Spirit who was given to us.
ROMANS 5:5 NKJV

And now you Gentiles have also heard the truth, the Good News
that God saves you. And when you believed in Christ, he identified
you as his own by giving you the Holy Spirit, whom he promised
long ago. **EPHESIANS 1:13 NLT**

But Christ has blessed you with the Holy Spirit. Now the Spirit stays
in you, and you don't need any teachers. The Spirit is truthful and
teaches you everything. So stay one in your heart with Christ, just
as the Spirit has taught you to do. **1 JOHN 2:27 CEV**

…Christ has *blessed*
you with the
Holy Spirit.

Honor

(high regard; high position)

Yours, LORD, is the greatness and the power and the glory and the majesty and the splendor, for everything in heaven and earth is yours. Yours, LORD, is the kingdom; you are exalted as head over all. Wealth and honor come from you; you are the ruler of all things. In your hands are strength and power to exalt and give strength to all. Now, our God, we give you thanks, and praise your glorious name. 1 CHRONICLES 29:11–13 NIV

I have a lot of enemies, LORD. Many fight against me and say, "God won't rescue you!" But you are my shield, and you give me victory and great honor. PSALM 3:1–3 CEV

For the LORD God is a sun and shield; the LORD bestows favor and honor; no good thing does he withhold from those whose walk is blameless. PSALM 84:11 NIV

The reward for humility and fear of the LORD is riches and honor and life. PROVERBS 22:4 ESV

And now the LORD speaks—the one who formed me in my mother's womb to be his servant, who commissioned me to bring Israel back to him. The LORD has honored me, and my God has given me strength. ISAIAH 49:5 NLT

"At that time I will deal with all who oppressed you. I will rescue the lame; I will gather the exiles. I will give them praise and honor in

every land where they have suffered shame. At that time I will gather you; at that time I will bring you home. I will give you honor and praise among all the peoples of the earth when I restore your fortunes before your very eyes," says the LORD.
ZEPHANIAH 3:19-20 NIV

Therefore anyone who sets aside one of the least of these commands and teaches others accordingly will be called least in the kingdom of heaven, but whoever practices and teaches these commands will be called great in the kingdom of heaven. MATTHEW 5:19 NIV

He will give eternal life to those who keep on doing good, seeking after the glory and honor and immortality that God offers.
ROMANS 2:7 NLT

Your faith will be like gold that has been tested in a fire. And these trials will prove that your faith is worth much more than gold that can be destroyed. They will show that you will be given praise and honor and glory when Jesus Christ returns. 1 PETER 1:7 CEV

Hope

(a positive expectation that what is wanted will happen)

"For I know the plans I have for you," declares the LORD, "plans to prosper you and not to harm you, plans to give you hope and a future." JEREMIAH 29:11 NIV

Even when there was no reason for hope, Abraham kept hoping—believing that he would become the father of many nations. For God had said to him, "That's how many descendants you will have!" ROMANS 4:18 NLT

Such things were written in the Scriptures long ago to teach us. And the Scriptures give us hope and encouragement as we wait patiently for God's promises to be fulfilled. ROMANS 15:4 NLT

I pray that God, who gives hope, will bless you with complete happiness and peace because of your faith. And may the power of the Holy Spirit fill you with hope. ROMANS 15:13 CEV

I pray that your hearts will be flooded with light so that you can understand the confident hope he has given to those he called—his holy people who are his rich and glorious inheritance. EPHESIANS 1:18 NLT

All of you are part of the same body. There is only one Spirit of God, just as you were given one hope when you were chosen to be God's people. EPHESIANS 4:4 CEV

"And his name will be the hope of all the world." MATTHEW 12:21 NLT

God also bound himself with an oath, so that those who received the promise could be perfectly sure that he would never change his mind. So God has given both his promise and his oath. These two things are unchangeable because it is impossible for God to lie. Therefore, we who have fled to him for refuge can have great confidence as we hold to the hope that lies before us. This hope is a strong and trustworthy anchor for our souls. It leads us through the curtain into God's inner sanctuary. Jesus has already gone in there for us. He has become our eternal High Priest in the order of Melchizedek. HEBREWS 6:17-20 NLT

Praise be to the God and Father of our Lord Jesus Christ! In his great mercy he has given us new birth into a living hope through the resurrection of Jesus Christ from the dead . . . 1 PETER 1:3 NIV

But in your hearts revere Christ as Lord. Always be prepared to give an answer to everyone who asks you to give the reason for the hope that you have. But do this with gentleness and respect . . . 1 PETER 3:15 NIV

Identity

*(who a person is; characteristics by which
a person is recognized)*

And the LORD has declared this day that you are his people, his treasured possession as he promised, and that you are to keep all his commands. DEUTERONOMY 26:18 NIV

But now, this is what the LORD says—he who created you, Jacob, he who formed you, Israel: "Do not fear, for I have redeemed you; I have summoned you by name; you are mine." ISAIAH 43:1 NIV

"They will be my people, and I will be their God." JEREMIAH 32:38 NIV

"I tell you, love your enemies. Help and give without expecting a return. You'll never—I promise—regret it. Live out this God-created identity the way our Father lives toward us, generously and graciously, even when we're at our worst. Our Father is kind; you be kind." LUKE 6:35-36 MSG

"Your love for one another will prove to the world that you are my disciples." JOHN 13:35 NLT

For his Spirit joins with our spirit to affirm that we are God's children. ROMANS 8:16 NLT

For none of us lives for ourselves alone, and none of us dies for ourselves alone. If we live, we live for the Lord; and if we die, we die for the Lord. So, whether we live or die, we belong to the Lord. For this very reason, Christ died and returned to life so that he might be the Lord of both the dead and the living. ROMANS 14:7–9 NIV

Now it is God who makes both us and you stand firm in Christ. He anointed us, set his seal of ownership on us, and put his Spirit in our hearts as a deposit, guaranteeing what is to come.
2 CORINTHIANS 1:21–22 NIV

My old self has been crucified with Christ. It is no longer I who live, but Christ lives in me. So I live in this earthly body by trusting in the Son of God, who loved me and gave himself for me.
GALATIANS 2:20 NLT

So now you Gentiles are no longer strangers and foreigners. You are citizens along with all of God's holy people. You are members of God's family. Together, we are his house, built on the foundation of the apostles and the prophets. And the cornerstone is Christ Jesus himself. EPHESIANS 2:19–20 NLT

But you are not like that, for you are a chosen people. You are royal priests, a holy nation, God's very own possession. As a result, you can show others the goodness of God, for he called you out of the darkness into his wonderful light. "Once you had no identity as a people; now you are God's people. Once you received no mercy; now you have received God's mercy." 1 PETER 2:9–10 NLT

And they will see his face, and his name will be written on their foreheads. REVELATION 22:4 NLT

Inheritance

(to receive a bequest as a result of being an heir)

God blesses those who are humble, for they will inherit the whole earth. MATTHEW 5:5 NLT

"And now I entrust you to God and the message of his grace that is able to build you up and give you an inheritance with all those he has set apart for himself." ACTS 20:32 NLT

This resurrection life you received from God is not a timid, grave-tending life. It's adventurously expectant, greeting God with a childlike "What's next, Papa?" God's Spirit touches our spirits and confirms who we really are. We know who he is, and we know who we are: Father and children. And we know we are going to get what's coming to us—an unbelievable inheritance! We go through exactly what Christ goes through. If we go through the hard times with him, then we're certainly going to go through the good times with him! ROMANS 8:15–17 MSG

Furthermore, because we are united with Christ, we have received an inheritance from God, for he chose us in advance, and he makes everything work out according to his plan. EPHESIANS 1:11 NLT

The Spirit is God's guarantee that he will give us the inheritance he promised and that he has purchased us to be his own people. He did this so we would praise and glorify him. EPHESIANS 1:14 NLT

Work willingly at whatever you do, as though you were working for the Lord rather than for people. Remember that the Lord will give you an inheritance as your reward, and that the Master you are serving is Christ. COLOSSIANS 3:23–24 NLT

For this reason Christ is the mediator of a new covenant, that those who are called may receive the promised eternal inheritance—now that he has died as a ransom to set them free from the sins committed under the first covenant. HEBREWS 9:15 NIV

Like a will that takes effect when someone dies, the new covenant was put into action at Jesus' death. His death marked the transition from the old plan to the new one, canceling the old obligations and accompanying sins, and summoning the heirs to receive the eternal inheritance that was promised them. He brought together God and his people in this new way. HEBREWS 9:16–17 MSG

All praise to God, the Father of our Lord Jesus Christ. It is by his great mercy that we have been born again, because God raised Jesus Christ from the dead. Now we live with great expectation, and we have a priceless inheritance—an inheritance that is kept in heaven for you, pure and undefiled, beyond the reach of change and decay. And through your faith, God is protecting you by his power until you receive this salvation, which is ready to be revealed on the last day for all to see. 1 PETER 1:3–5 NLT

Instructions

*(information given or taught; command or order;
details on procedure)*

Jesus sent out the twelve apostles with these instructions: "Don't go
to the Gentiles or the Samaritans, but only to the people of Israel—
God's lost sheep. Go and announce to them that the Kingdom
of Heaven is near. Heal the sick, raise the dead, cure those with
leprosy, and cast out demons. Give as freely as you have received!"
... When Jesus had finished giving these instructions to his twelve
disciples, he went out to teach and preach in towns throughout
the region. MATTHEW 10:5-8, 11:1 NLT

Jesus replied: "'Love the Lord your God with all your heart and
with all your soul and with all your mind.' This is the first and
greatest commandment. And the second is like it: 'Love your
neighbor as yourself.' All the Law and the Prophets hang on these
two commandments." MATTHEW 22:37-40 NIV

The Lord now chose seventy-two other disciples and sent them
ahead in pairs to all the towns and places he planned to visit. These
were his instructions to them: "The harvest is great, but the workers
are few. So pray to the Lord who is in charge of the harvest; ask
him to send more workers into his fields. Now go, and remember
that I am sending you out as lambs among wolves." LUKE 10:1-3 NLT

In my former book, Theophilus, I wrote about all that Jesus began
to do and to teach until the day he was taken up to heaven, after
giving instructions through the Holy Spirit to the apostles he
had chosen. After his suffering, he presented himself to them and

gave many convincing proofs that he was alive. He appeared to them over a period of forty days and spoke about the kingdom of God. On one occasion, while he was eating with them, he gave them this command: "Do not leave Jerusalem, but wait for the gift my Father promised, which you have heard me speak about. For John baptized with water, but in a few days you will be baptized with the Holy Spirit." ACTS 1:1–5 NIV

Let me go over with you again exactly what goes on in the Lord's Supper and why it is so centrally important. I received my instructions from the Master himself and passed them on to you. The Master, Jesus, on the night of his betrayal, took bread. Having given thanks, he broke it and said, "This is my body, broken for you. Do this to remember me." After supper, he did the same thing with the cup: "This cup is my blood, my new covenant with you. Each time you drink this cup, remember me." What you must solemnly realize is that every time you eat this bread and every time you drink this cup, you reenact in your words and actions the death of the Master. You will be drawn back to this meal again and again until the Master returns. You must never let familiarity breed contempt. 1 CORINTHIANS 11:23–26 MSG

Fathers, do not exasperate your children; instead, bring them up in the training and instruction of the Lord. EPHESIANS 6:4 NIV

All Scripture *is* given by inspiration of God, and *is* profitable for doctrine, for reproof, for correction, for instruction in righteousness, that the man of God may be complete, thoroughly equipped for every good work. 2 TIMOTHY 3:16–17 NKJV

Intercession

(mediation; prayer on behalf of another; negotiator who acts as a link between parties)

Then people brought little children to Jesus for him to place his hands on them and pray for them. MATTHEW 19:13 NIV

Jesus said, "Father, forgive them, for they do not know what they are doing." And they divided up his clothes by casting lots. LUKE 23:34 NIV

My dear children, I am writing this to you so that you will not sin. But if anyone does sin, we have an advocate who pleads our case before the Father. He is Jesus Christ, the one who is truly righteous. 1 JOHN 2:1 NLT

Who *is* he who condemns? *It is* Christ who died, and furthermore is also risen, who is even at the right hand of God, who also makes intercession for us. ROMANS 8:34 NKJV

For *there is* one God and one Mediator between God and men, *the* Man Christ Jesus, who gave Himself a ransom for all, to be testified in due time . . . 1 TIMOTHY 2:5–6 NKJV

Therefore He is also able to save to the uttermost those who come to God through Him, since He always lives to make intercession for them. HEBREWS 7:25 NKJV

But now Jesus, our High Priest, has been given a ministry that is far superior to the old priesthood, for he is the one who mediates

❧ *continued* ❧

for us a far better covenant with God, based on better promises.
HEBREWS 8:6 NLT

For this reason Christ is the mediator of a new covenant, that those who are called may receive the promised eternal inheritance—now that he has died as a ransom to set them free from the sins committed under the first covenant. **HEBREWS 9:15 NIV**

And you are living stones that God is building into his spiritual temple. What's more, you are his holy priests. Through the mediation of Jesus Christ, you offer spiritual sacrifices that please God. **1 PETER 2:5 NLT**

Through the *mediation*
of *Jesus Christ,*
you offer spiritual
sacrifices that
please God.

Intimacy

(personal; closely acquainted; familiar)

Yet I am always with you; you hold me by my right hand. You guide me with your counsel, and afterward you will take me into glory.
PSALM 73:23–24 NIV

The LORD is close to all who call on him, yes, to all who call on him in truth. He grants the desires of those who fear him; he hears their cries for help and rescues them. PSALM 145:18–19 NLT

People of Israel, I have chosen you as my servant. I am your Creator. You were in my care even before you were born. Israel, don't be terrified! You are my chosen servant, my very favorite.
ISAIAH 44:1-2 CEV

"Then when you call, the LORD will answer. 'Yes, I am here,' he will quickly reply." ISAIAH 58:9 NLT

I will answer them before they even call to me. While they are still talking about their needs, I will go ahead and answer their prayers!
ISAIAH 65:24 NLT

"Look! The virgin will conceive a child! She will give birth to a son, and they will call him Immanuel, which means 'God is with us.'" MATTHEW 1:23 NLT

And I am convinced that nothing can ever separate us from God's love. Neither death nor life, neither angels nor demons, neither our fears for today nor our worries about tomorrow—not even the powers of hell can separate us from God's love. No power in the sky above or in the earth below—indeed, nothing in all creation will ever be able to separate us from the love of God that is revealed in Christ Jesus our Lord. ROMANS 8:38–39 NLT

But now you have been united with Christ Jesus. Once you were far away from God, but now you have been brought near to him through the blood of Christ. EPHESIANS 2:13 NLT

The amazing grace of the Master, Jesus Christ, the extravagant love of God, the intimate friendship of the Holy Spirit, be with all of you. 2 CORINTHIANS 13:14 MSG

This is how we know we're living steadily and deeply in him, and he in us: He's given us life from his life, from his very own Spirit. Also, we've seen for ourselves and continue to state openly that the Father sent his Son as Savior of the world. Everyone who confesses that Jesus is God's Son participates continuously in an intimate relationship with God. We know it so well, we've embraced it heart and soul, this love that comes from God. 1 JOHN 4:13–16 MSG

Come near to God and he will come near to you. JAMES 4:8 NIV

Joy

(delight; rejoicing)

For His anger *is but for* a moment, His favor *is for* life; Weeping may endure for a night, But joy *comes* in the morning.
PSALM 30:5 NKJV

God gives wisdom, knowledge, and joy to those who please him. But if a sinner becomes wealthy, God takes the wealth away and gives it to those who please him. This, too, is meaningless—like chasing the wind. **ECCLESIASTES 2:26 NLT**

After looking at the way things are on this earth, here's what I've decided is the best way to live: Take care of yourself, have a good time, and make the most of whatever job you have for as long as God gives you life. And that's about it. That's the human lot. Yes, we should make the most of what God gives, both the bounty and the capacity to enjoy it, accepting what's given and delighting in the work. It's God's gift! God deals out joy in the present, the *now*. It's useless to brood over how long we might live.
ECCLESIASTES 5:18-20 MSG

The humble will be filled with fresh joy from the LORD. The poor will rejoice in the Holy One of Israel. **ISAIAH 29:19 NLT**

Nehemiah said, "Go and enjoy choice food and sweet drinks, and send some to those who have nothing prepared. This day is holy to our Lord. Do not grieve, for the joy of the LORD is your strength."
NEHEMIAH 8:10 NIV

"Now I am coming to you. I told them many things while I was with them in this world so they would be filled with my joy."
JOHN 17:13 NLT

"'You have made known to me the paths of life; you will fill me with joy in your presence.'" **ACTS 2:28 NIV**

May the God of hope fill you with all joy and peace in believing, so that by the power of the Holy Spirit you may abound in hope.
ROMANS 15:13 ESV

But the fruit of the Spirit is love, joy, peace, forbearance, kindness, goodness, faithfulness, gentleness and self-control. Against such things there is no law. **GALATIANS 5:22–23 NIV**

Instruct those who are rich in this present world not to be conceited or to fix their hope on the uncertainty of riches, but on God, who richly supplies us with all things to enjoy. **1 TIMOTHY 6:17 NASB**

Offer praise to God our Savior because of our Lord Jesus Christ! Only God can keep you from falling and make you pure and joyful in his glorious presence. Before time began and now and forevermore, God is worthy of glory, honor, power, and authority. Amen.
JUDE 1:24–25 CEV

Justice

(to reward or penalize as deserved)

Don't say, "I will get even for this wrong." Wait for the LORD to handle the matter. PROVERBS 20:22 NLT

He will give justice to the poor and make fair decisions for the exploited. The earth will shake at the force of his word, and one breath from his mouth will destroy the wicked. ISAIAH 11:4 NLT

"Moreover, the Father judges no one, but has entrusted all judgment to the Son, that all may honor the Son just as they honor the Father. Whoever does not honor the Son does not honor the Father, who sent him. Very truly I tell you, whoever hears my word and believes him who sent me has eternal life and will not be judged but has crossed over from death to life. Very truly I tell you, a time is coming and has now come when the dead will hear the voice of the Son of God and those who hear will live. For as the Father has life in himself, so he has granted the Son also to have life in himself. And he has given him authority to judge because he is the Son of Man." JOHN 5:22–27 NIV

And he ordered us to preach everywhere and to testify that Jesus is the one appointed by God to be the judge of all—the living and the dead. ACTS 10:42 NLT

You may think you can condemn such people, but you are just as bad, and you have no excuse! When you say they are wicked and should be punished, you are condemning yourself, for you who judge others do these very same things. And we know that God, in his justice, will punish anyone who does such things. Since you judge others for doing these things, why do you think you can avoid God's judgment when you do the same things? ROMANS 2:1–3 NLT

But because of your stubbornness and your unrepentant heart, you are storing up wrath against yourself for the day of God's wrath, when his righteous judgment will be revealed. God "will repay each person according to what they have done." To those who by persistence in doing good seek glory, honor and immortality, he will give eternal life. But for those who are self-seeking and who reject the truth and follow evil, there will be wrath and anger. There will be trouble and distress for every human being who does evil: first for the Jew, then for the Gentile; but glory, honor and peace for everyone who does good: first for the Jew, then for the Gentile. For God does not show favoritism. All who sin apart from the law will also perish apart from the law, and all who sin under the law will be judged by the law. For it is not those who hear the law who are righteous in God's sight, but it is those who obey the law who will be declared righteous. ROMANS 2:5–13 NIV

For we must all stand before Christ to be judged. We will each receive whatever we deserve for the good or evil we have done in this earthly body. 2 CORINTHIANS 5:10 NLT

Justification

(to show to be right or fair; to show an adequate reason for something done; to declare to be righteous)

He was delivered over to death for our sins and was raised to life for our justification. Therefore, since we have been justified through faith, we have peace with God through our Lord Jesus Christ, through whom we have gained access by faith into this grace in which we now stand. And we boast in the hope of the glory of God. ROMANS 4:25–5:2 NIV

Since we have now been justified by his blood, how much more shall we be saved from God's wrath through him! For if, while we were God's enemies, we were reconciled to him through the death of his Son, how much more, having been reconciled, shall we be saved through his life! Not only is this so, but we also boast in God through our Lord Jesus Christ, through whom we have now received reconciliation. Therefore, just as sin entered the world through one man, and death through sin, and in this way death came to all people, because all sinned—To be sure, sin was in the world before the law was given, but sin is not charged against anyone's account where there is no law. Nevertheless, death reigned from the time of Adam to the time of Moses, even over those who did not sin by breaking a command, as did Adam, who is a pattern of the one to come. But the gift is not like the trespass. For if the many died by the trespass of the one man, how much more did God's grace and the gift that came by the grace of the one man, Jesus Christ, overflow to the many! Nor can the gift of God be compared with the result of one man's sin: The judgment followed one sin and brought condemnation, but the gift followed many trespasses and brought justification. For if, by the trespass of the one man, death reigned through that one man, how much more will those who receive God's abundant provision of grace and of the gift of righteousness reign in life through the one man, Jesus Christ! Consequently, just as one trespass resulted in condemnation for all people, so also one righteous act resulted in justification and life for all people. For just as through the disobedience of the one man the many were made sinners, so also through the obedience of the one man the many will be made righteous. The law was brought in so that the trespass might increase. But where sin increased, grace increased all the more, so that, just as sin reigned in death, so also grace might reign through righteousness to bring eternal life through Jesus Christ our Lord. ROMANS 5:9–21 NIV

And we know that in all things God works for the good of those who love him, who have been called according to his purpose. For those God foreknew he also predestined to be conformed to the image of his Son, that he might be the firstborn among many brothers and sisters. And those he predestined, he also called; those he called, he also justified; those he justified, he also glorified. ROMANS 8:28–30 NIV

"We who are Jews by birth and not sinful Gentiles know that a person is not justified by the works of the law, but by faith in Jesus Christ. So we, too, have put our faith in Christ Jesus that we may be justified by faith in Christ and not by the works of the law, because by the works of the law no one will be justified." GALATIANS 2:15–16 NIV

Kindness

(friendly; tenderhearted; generous)

The LORD answered: "All right. I am the LORD, and I show mercy and kindness to anyone I choose. I will let you see my glory and hear my holy name . . ." EXODUS 33:19 CEV

The LORD God is kind and merciful, and if you turn back to him, he will no longer turn his back on you. 2 CHRONICLES 30:9 CEV

Your anger lasts a little while, but your kindness lasts for a lifetime. At night we may cry, but when morning comes we will celebrate. PSALM 30:5 CEV

"God's love and kindness will shine upon us like the sun that rises in the sky." LUKE 1:78 CEV

The Law was given by Moses, but Jesus Christ brought us undeserved kindness and truth. JOHN 1:17 CEV

"But I don't care what happens to me, as long as I finish the work that the Lord Jesus gave me to do. And that work is to tell the good news about God's great kindness." ACTS 20:24 CEV

Don't you see how wonderfully kind, tolerant, and patient God is with you? Does this mean nothing to you? Can't you see that his kindness is intended to turn you from your sin? ROMANS 2:4 NLT

Yet God, with undeserved kindness, declares that we are righteous.

᭒ *continued* ᭒

He did this through Christ Jesus when he freed us from the penalty for our sins. ROMANS 3:24 NLT

But the fruit of the Spirit is love, joy, peace, forbearance, kindness, goodness, faithfulness, gentleness and self-control. Against such things there is no law. GALATIANS 5:22–23 NIV

Be kind and compassionate to one another, forgiving each other, just as in Christ God forgave you. EPHESIANS 4:32 NIV

God saved us and chose us to be his holy people. We did nothing to deserve this, but God planned it because he is so kind. Even before time began God planned for Christ Jesus to show kindness to us. Now Christ Jesus has come to show us the kindness of God. Christ our Savior defeated death and brought us the good news. It shines like a light and offers life that never ends. 2 TIMOTHY 1:9–10 CEV

Now *Christ Jesus*
has come to show us
the *kindness of God.*

∽ *Day 58* ∽

Kingdom of Heaven

(the spiritual realm of God)

"Blessed are the poor in spirit, for theirs is the kingdom of heaven…
Blessed are those who are persecuted because of righteousness,
for theirs is the kingdom of heaven." **MATTHEW 5:3, 10 NIV**

"Not everyone who says to me, 'Lord, Lord,' will enter the kingdom
of heaven, but only the one who does the will of my Father who is
in heaven." **MATTHEW 7:21 NIV**

"And I will give you the keys of the Kingdom of Heaven. Whatever
you forbid on earth will be forbidden in heaven, and whatever you
permit on earth will be permitted in heaven." **MATTHEW 16:19 NLT**

At that time the disciples came to Jesus and asked, "Who, then,
is the greatest in the kingdom of heaven?" He called a little child
to him, and placed the child among them. And he said: "Truly I
tell you, unless you change and become like little children, you
will never enter the kingdom of heaven. Therefore, whoever takes
the lowly position of this child is the greatest in the kingdom of
heaven." **MATTHEW 18:1–4 NIV**

"But don't rejoice because evil spirits obey you; rejoice because
your names are registered in heaven." **LUKE 10:20 NLT**

"Do not fear, little flock, for it is your Father's good pleasure
to give you the kingdom." **LUKE 12:32 NKJV**

continued

You have stayed with me in my time of trial. And just as my Father has granted me a Kingdom, I now grant you the right to eat and drink at my table in my Kingdom. And you will sit on thrones, judging the twelve tribes of Israel. LUKE 22:28–30 NLT

My Father's house has many rooms; if that were not so, would I have told you that I am going there to prepare a place for you? And if I go and prepare a place for you, I will come back and take you to be with me that you also may be where I am. JOHN 14:2–3 NIV

My dear friends, pay attention. God has given a lot of faith to the poor people in this world. He has also promised them a share in his kingdom that he will give to everyone who loves him. JAMES 2:5 CEV

He has also
promised them a share
in *his kingdom* . . .

Kinship

(family relationship)

Blessed are the peacemakers, for they will be called children of God. MATTHEW 5:9 NIV

While Jesus was still talking to the crowd, his mother and brothers stood outside, wanting to speak to him. Someone told him, "Your mother and brothers are standing outside, wanting to speak to you." He replied to him, "Who is my mother, and who are my brothers?" Pointing to his disciples, he said, "Here are my mother and my brothers. For whoever does the will of my Father in heaven is my brother and sister and mother." MATTHEW 12:46–50 NIV

But to all who believed him and accepted him, he gave the right to become children of God. JOHN 1:12 NLT

For all who are led by the Spirit of God are children of God. ROMANS 8:14 NLT

For you are all children of God through faith in Christ Jesus. GALATIANS 3:26 NLT

Behold what manner of love the Father has bestowed on us, that we should be called children of God! Therefore the world does not know us, because it did not know Him. Beloved, now we are children of God; and it has not yet been revealed what we shall be, but we know that when He is revealed, we shall be like Him, for we shall see Him as He is. 1 JOHN 3:1–2 NKJV

Knowledge

(acquaintance with facts, truths, or principles; awareness of fact; mental apprehension)

My son, if you accept my words and store up my commands within you, turning your ear to wisdom and applying your heart to understanding—indeed, if you call out for insight and cry aloud for understanding, and if you look for it as for silver and search for it as for hidden treasure, then you will understand the fear of the LORD and find the knowledge of God. For the LORD gives wisdom; from his mouth come knowledge and understanding. PROVERBS 2:1–6 NIV

To these four young men God gave knowledge and understanding of all kinds of literature and learning. And Daniel could understand visions and dreams of all kinds. DANIEL 1:17 NIV

To those who listen to my teaching, more understanding will be given, and they will have an abundance of knowledge. But for those who are not listening, even what little understanding they have will be taken away from them. MATTHEW 13:12 NLT

He said, "The knowledge of the secrets of the kingdom of God has been given to you, but to others I speak in parables, so that, 'though seeing, they may not see; though hearing, they may not understand.'" LUKE 8:10 NIV

For in him you have been enriched in every way—with all kinds of speech and with all knowledge—God thus confirming our testimony about Christ among you. 1 CORINTHIANS 1:5–6 NIV

continued

To one person the Spirit gives the ability to give wise advice; to another the same Spirit gives a message of special knowledge. **1 CORINTHIANS 12:8 NLT**

For God, who said, "Let light shine out of darkness," made his light shine in our hearts to give us the light of the knowledge of God's glory displayed in the face of Christ. **2 CORINTHIANS 4:6 NIV**

I have not stopped thanking God for you. I pray for you constantly, asking God, the glorious Father of our Lord Jesus Christ, to give you spiritual wisdom and insight so that you might grow in your knowledge of God. **EPHESIANS 1:16–17 NLT**

...to give you spiritual *wisdom and insight* so that you might grow in your *knowledge of God.*

Life, Eternal

(without beginning or end; to have life for all time)

"No one has ever gone into heaven except the one who came from heaven—the Son of Man. Just as Moses lifted up the snake in the wilderness, so the Son of Man must be lifted up, that everyone who believes may have eternal life in him." For God so loved the world that he gave his one and only Son, that whoever believes in him shall not perish but have eternal life. For God did not send his Son into the world to condemn the world, but to save the world through him . . . Whoever believes in the Son has eternal life, but whoever rejects the Son will not see life, for God's wrath remains on them. JOHN 3:13–17, 36 NIV

"I tell you the truth, anyone who obeys my teaching will never die!" JOHN 8:51 NLT

Jesus said to her, "I am the resurrection and the life. The one who believes in me will live, even though they die; and whoever lives by believing in me will never die. Do you believe this?" JOHN 11:25–26 NIV

After Jesus said this, he looked toward heaven and prayed: "Father, the hour has come. Glorify your Son, that your Son may glorify you. For you granted him authority over all people that he might give eternal life to all those you have given him. Now this is eternal life: that they know you, the only true God, and Jesus Christ, whom you have sent. I have brought you glory on earth by finishing the work you gave me to do. And now, Father, glorify me in your

presence with the glory I had with you before the world began."
JOHN 17:1–5 NIV

For the wages of sin is death, but the gift of God is eternal life in
Christ Jesus our Lord. ROMANS 6:23 NIV

The world and its desires pass away, but whoever does the will of
God lives forever... And this is what he promised us—eternal life.
1 JOHN 2:17, 25 NIV

God showed how much he loved us by sending his one and only
Son into the world so that we might have eternal life through him.
1 JOHN 4:9 NLT

And this is the testimony: God has given us eternal life, and this
life is in his Son. Whoever has the Son has life; whoever does not
have the Son of God does not have life. I write these things to you
who believe in the name of the Son of God so that you may know
that you have eternal life. 1 JOHN 5:11–13 NIV

Life, New

*(death of the sinful nature and rebirth
into a spiritual creation)*

Yes, Adam's one sin brings condemnation for everyone, but Christ's one act of righteousness brings a right relationship with God and new life for everyone. ROMANS 5:18 NLT

For we died and were buried with Christ by baptism. And just as Christ was raised from the dead by the glorious power of the Father, now we also may live new lives. Since we have been united with him in his death, we will also be raised to life as he was. We know that our old sinful selves were crucified with Christ so that sin might lose its power in our lives. We are no longer slaves to sin. For when we died with Christ we were set free from the power of sin. And since we died with Christ, we know we will also live with him. We are sure of this because Christ was raised from the dead, and he will never die again. Death no longer has any power over him. When he died, he died once to break the power of sin. But now that he lives, he lives for the glory of God. So you also should consider yourselves to be dead to the power of sin and alive to God through Christ Jesus. Do not let sin control the way you live; do not give in to sinful desires. Do not let any part of your body become an instrument of evil to serve sin. Instead, give yourselves completely to God, for you were dead, but now you have new life. ROMANS 6:4–13 NLT

Either way, Christ's love controls us. Since we believe that Christ died for all, we also believe that we have all died to our old life. He died for everyone so that those who receive his new life will no

longer live for themselves. Instead, they will live for Christ, who died and was raised for them. So we have stopped evaluating others from a human point of view. At one time we thought of Christ merely from a human point of view. How differently we know him now! This means that anyone who belongs to Christ has become a new person. The old life is gone; a new life has begun!
2 CORINTHIANS 5:14–17 NLT

Those who belong to Christ Jesus have nailed the passions and desires of their sinful nature to his cross and crucified them there.
GALATIANS 5:24 NLT

For you were buried with Christ when you were baptized. And with him you were raised to new life because you trusted the mighty power of God, who raised Christ from the dead. **COLOSSIANS 2:12 NLT**

". . . he saved us, not because of the righteous things we had done, but because of his mercy. He washed away our sins, giving us a new birth and new life through the Holy Spirit." **TITUS 3:5 NLT**

Light

(God; spiritual illumination; inspiration; knowledge)

Light shines on the righteous and joy on the upright in heart.
PSALM 97:11 NIV

"You are the light of the world. A town built on a hill cannot be
hidden. Neither do people light a lamp and put it under a bowl.
Instead they put it on its stand, and it gives light to everyone in
the house. In the same way, let your light shine before others, that
they may see your good deeds and glorify your Father in heaven."
MATTHEW 5:14–16 NIV

In the beginning was the Word, and the Word was with God, and
the Word was God. He was with God in the beginning. Through
him all things were made; without him nothing was made that
has been made. In him was life, and that life was the light of all
mankind. The light shines in the darkness, and the darkness has
not overcome it. There was a man sent from God whose name was
John. He came as a witness to testify concerning that light, so that
through him all might believe. He himself was not the light; he
came only as a witness to the light. The true light that gives light
to everyone was coming into the world. **JOHN 1:1–9 NIV**

When Jesus spoke again to the people, he said, "I am the light of
the world. Whoever follows me will never walk in darkness, but
will have the light of life." **JOHN 8:12 NIV**

I have come into the world as a light, so that no one who believes in me should stay in darkness. JOHN 12:46 NIV

For God, who said, "Let light shine out of darkness," made his light shine in our hearts to give us the light of the knowledge of God's glory displayed in the face of Christ. 2 CORINTHIANS 4:6 NIV

For once you were full of darkness, but now you have light from the Lord. So live as people of light! EPHESIANS 5:8 NLT

But all things that are exposed are made manifest by the light, for whatever makes manifest is light. Therefore He says: "Awake, you who sleep, Arise from the dead, And Christ will give you light." EPHESIANS 5:13–14 NKJV

This is the message we heard from Jesus and now declare to you: God is light, and there is no darkness in him at all. So we are lying if we say we have fellowship with God but go on living in spiritual darkness; we are not practicing the truth. But if we are living in the light, as God is in the light, then we have fellowship with each other, and the blood of Jesus, his Son, cleanses us from all sin. 1 JOHN 1:5–7 NLT

Likeness

(similar in appearance or nature)

Then God said, "Let us make mankind in our image, in our likeness, so that they may rule over the fish in the sea and the birds in the sky, over the livestock and all the wild animals, and over all the creatures that move along the ground." **GENESIS 1:26 NIV**

As for me, I will see Your face in righteousness; I shall be satisfied when I awake in Your likeness. **PSALM 17:15 NKJV**

Therefore we were buried with Him through baptism into death, that just as Christ was raised from the dead by the glory of the Father, even so we also should walk in newness of life. For if we have been united together in the likeness of His death, certainly we also shall be *in the likeness* of *His* resurrection, knowing this, that our old man was crucified with *Him*, that the body of sin might be done away with, that we should no longer be slaves of sin. **ROMANS 6:4–6 NKJV**

For what the law was powerless to do because it was weakened by the flesh, God did by sending his own Son in the likeness of sinful flesh to be a sin offering. And so he condemned sin in the flesh. **ROMANS 8:3 NIV**

A man should not wear anything on his head when worshiping, for man is made in God's image and reflects God's glory.
1 CORINTHIANS 11:7 NLT

As was the earthly man, so are those who are of the earth; and as is the heavenly man, so also are those who are of heaven. And just as we have borne the image of the earthly man, so shall we bear the image of the heavenly man. 1 CORINTHIANS 15:48–49 NIV

The god of this age has blinded the minds of unbelievers, so that they cannot see the light of the gospel that displays the glory of Christ, who is the image of God. 2 CORINTHIANS 4:4 NIV

And we all, who with unveiled faces contemplate the Lord's glory, are being transformed into his image with ever-increasing glory, which comes from the Lord, who is the Spirit. 2 CORINTHIANS 3:18 NIV

Christ is the visible image of the invisible God. He existed before anything was created and is supreme over all creation.
COLOSSIANS 1:15 NLT

Christ is the *visible*
image of the
invisible God.

Living Water

(the never-ending spiritual life, healing, refreshment and nourishment found only in the person of Christ)

"For my people have done two evil things: They have abandoned me—the fountain of living water. And they have dug for themselves cracked cisterns that can hold no water at all!" JEREMIAH 2:13 NLT

Now he had to go through Samaria. So he came to a town in Samaria called Sychar, near the plot of ground Jacob had given to his son Joseph. Jacob's well was there, and Jesus, tired as he was from the journey, sat down by the well. It was about noon. When a Samaritan woman came to draw water, Jesus said to her, "Will you give me a drink?" (His disciples had gone into the town to buy food.) The Samaritan woman said to him, "You are a Jew and I am a Samaritan woman. How can you ask me for a drink?" (For Jews do not associate with Samaritans.) Jesus answered her, "If you knew the gift of God and who it is that asks you for a drink, you would have asked him and he would have given you living water." "Sir," the woman said, "you have nothing to draw with and the well is deep. Where can you get this living water? Are you greater than our father Jacob, who gave us the well and drank from it himself, as did also his sons and his livestock?"Jesus answered, "Everyone who drinks this water will be thirsty again, but whoever drinks the water I give them will never thirst. Indeed, the water I give them will become in them a spring of water welling up to eternal life." JOHN 4:4–14 NIV

On the last day, the climax of the festival, Jesus stood and shouted to the crowds, "Anyone who is thirsty may come to me! Anyone

continued

who believes in me may come and drink! For the Scriptures declare, 'Rivers of living water will flow from his heart.'" (When he said "living water," he was speaking of the Spirit, who would be given to everyone believing in him. But the Spirit had not yet been given, because Jesus had not yet entered into his glory.)
JOHN 7:37–39 NLT

"'Never again will they hunger; never again will they thirst. The sun will not beat down on them,' nor any scorching heat. For the Lamb at the center of the throne will be their shepherd; 'he will lead them to springs of living water. And God will wipe away every tear from their eyes.'" REVELATION 7:16–17 NIV

"*"Never again* will they hunger; never again *will they thirst.*""

Longevity

(long life)

Stay on the path that the LORD your God has commanded you to follow. Then you will live long and prosperous lives in the land you are about to enter and occupy. DEUTERONOMY 5:33 NLT

These are the commands, decrees and laws the LORD your God directed me to teach you to observe in the land that you are crossing the Jordan to possess, so that you, your children and their children after them may fear the LORD your God as long as you live by keeping all his decrees and commands that I give you, and so that you may enjoy long life. DEUTERONOMY 6:1-2 NIV

"I will reward them with a long life and give them my salvation." PSALM 91:16 NLT

My child, never forget the things I have taught you. Store my commands in your heart. If you do this, you will live many years, and your life will be satisfying. PROVERBS 3:1-2 NLT

Listen, my son, accept what I say, and the years of your life will be many. PROVERBS 4:10 NIV

Wisdom will multiply your days and add years to your life. PROVERBS 9:11 NLT

The fear of the LORD adds length to life, but the years of the wicked are cut short. PROVERBS 10:27 NIV

True humility and fear of the LORD lead to riches, honor, and long life. PROVERBS 22:4 NLT

Stop taking advantage of foreigners, orphans, and widows. Don't kill innocent people. And stop worshiping other gods. Then I will let you enjoy a long life in this land I gave your ancestors. JEREMIAH 7:6–7 CEV

"This is how much God loved the world: He gave his Son, his one and only Son. And this is why: so that no one need be destroyed; by believing in him, anyone can have a whole and lasting life." JOHN 3:16 MSG

Children, do what your parents tell you. This is only right. "Honor your father and mother" is the first commandment that has a promise attached to it, namely, "so you will live well and have a long life." EPHESIANS 6:1–3 MSG

"… you will *live well* and have a *long life.*"

Love

(God's tender regard and concern for mankind; devotion; affection)

For God so loved the world that he gave his one and only Son, that whoever believes in him shall not perish but have eternal life. JOHN 3:16 NIV

Can anything ever separate us from Christ's love? Does it mean he no longer loves us if we have trouble or calamity, or are persecuted, or hungry, or destitute, or in danger, or threatened with death? (As the Scriptures say, "For your sake we are killed every day; we are being slaughtered like sheep.") No, despite all these things, overwhelming victory is ours through Christ, who loved us. And I am convinced that nothing can ever separate us from God's love. Neither death nor life, neither angels nor demons, neither our fears for today nor our worries about tomorrow—not even the powers of hell can separate us from God's love. No power in the sky above or in the earth below—indeed, nothing in all creation will ever be able to separate us from the love of God that is revealed in Christ Jesus our Lord. ROMANS 8:35–39 NLT

Love is patient, love is kind. It does not envy, it does not boast, it is not proud. It does not dishonor others, it is not self-seeking, it is not easily angered, it keeps no record of wrongs. Love does not delight in evil but rejoices with the truth. It always protects, always trusts, always hopes, always perseveres. Love never fails.
1 CORINTHIANS 13:4–8 NIV

Then Christ will make his home in your hearts as you trust in him.

continued

Your roots will grow down into God's love and keep you strong. And may you have the power to understand, as all God's people should, how wide, how long, how high, and how deep his love is. May you experience the love of Christ, though it is too great to understand fully. Then you will be made complete with all the fullness of life and power that comes from God. EPHESIANS 3:17–19 NLT

We know what real love is because Jesus gave up his life for us. So we also ought to give up our lives for our brothers and sisters. If someone has enough money to live well and sees a brother or sister in need but shows no compassion—how can God's love be in that person? Dear children, let's not merely say that we love each other; let us show the truth by our actions. Our actions will show that we belong to the truth, so we will be confident when we stand before God. Even if we feel guilty, God is greater than our feelings, and he knows everything. Dear friends, if we don't feel guilty, we can come to God with bold confidence. And we will receive from him whatever we ask because we obey him and do the things that please him. And this is his commandment: We must believe in the name of his Son, Jesus Christ, and love one another, just as he commanded us. Those who obey God's commandments remain in fellowship with him, and he with them. And we know he lives in us because the Spirit he gave us lives in us. 1 JOHN 3:16–24 NLT

Mercy

*(kindness in excess of what may be expected;
a disposition to forgive, pity, or be kind)*

And the LORD said, "I will cause all my goodness to pass in front of you, and I will proclaim my name, the LORD, in your presence. I will have mercy on whom I will have mercy, and I will have compassion on whom I will have compassion." EXODUS 33:19 NIV

Later, Matthew invited Jesus and his disciples to his home as dinner guests, along with many tax collectors and other disreputable sinners. But when the Pharisees saw this, they asked his disciples, "Why does your teacher eat with such scum?" When Jesus heard this, he said, "Healthy people don't need a doctor—sick people do." Then he added, "Now go and learn the meaning of this Scripture: 'I want you to show mercy, not offer sacrifices.' For I have come to call not those who think they are righteous, but those who know they are sinners." MATTHEW 9:10–13 NLT

As Jesus was getting into the boat, the man who had been demon-possessed begged to go with him. Jesus did not let him, but said, "Go home to your own people and tell them how much the Lord has done for you, and how he has had mercy on you."
MARK 5:18–19 NIV

He always shows mercy to everyone who worships him.
LUKE 1:50 CEV

Be merciful, just as your Father is merciful. LUKE 6:36 NIV

At one time you Gentiles rejected God. But now Israel has rejected God, and you have been shown mercy. And because of the mercy shown to you, they will also be shown mercy. All people have disobeyed God, and that's why he treats them as prisoners. But he does this, so that he can have mercy on all of them.
ROMANS 11:30–32 CEV

Even though I was once a blasphemer and a persecutor and a violent man, I was shown mercy because I acted in ignorance and unbelief. The grace of our Lord was poured out on me abundantly, along with the faith and love that are in Christ Jesus. Here is a trustworthy saying that deserves full acceptance: Christ Jesus came into the world to save sinners—of whom I am the worst. But for that very reason I was shown mercy so that in me, the worst of sinners, Christ Jesus might display his immense patience as an example for those who would believe in him and receive eternal life. 1 TIMOTHY 1:13–16 NIV

But when the kindness and love of God our Savior appeared, he saved us, not because of righteous things we had done, but because of his mercy. He saved us through the washing of rebirth and renewal by the Holy Spirit, whom he poured out on us generously through Jesus Christ our Savior, so that, having been justified by his grace, we might become heirs having the hope of eternal life. TITUS 3:4–7 NIV

"Once you had no identity as a people; now you are God's people. Once you received no mercy; now you have received God's mercy."
1 PETER 2:10 NLT

Obedience

(submission; willingness to follow instructions)

…But I gave them this command: Obey me, and I will be your God and you will be my people. Walk in obedience to all I command you, that it may go well with you. JEREMIAH 7:23 NIV

And I will put my Spirit in you so that you will follow my decrees and be careful to obey my regulations. EZEKIEL 36:27 NLT

Jesus responded, "Who do you think are my mother and brothers?" Looking around, taking in everyone seated around him, he said, "Right here, right in front of you—my mother and my brothers. Obedience is thicker than blood. The person who obeys God's will is my brother and sister and mother." MARK 3:33–35 MSG

When you obey my commandments, you remain in my love, just as I obey my Father's commandments and remain in his love. JOHN 15:10 NLT

For as by one man's disobedience many were made sinners, so also by one Man's obedience many will be made righteous. ROMANS 5:19 NKJV

Don't you know that when you offer yourselves to someone as obedient slaves, you are slaves of the one you obey—whether you are slaves to sin, which leads to death, or to obedience, which leads to righteousness? ROMANS 6:16 NIV

Now to him who is able to establish you in accordance with my gospel, the message I proclaim about Jesus Christ, in keeping with the revelation of the mystery hidden for long ages past, but now revealed and made known through the prophetic writings by the command of the eternal God, so that all the Gentiles might come to the obedience that comes from faith—to the only wise God be glory forever through Jesus Christ! Amen. **ROMANS 16:25–27 NIV**

For the weapons of our warfare *are* not carnal but mighty in God for pulling down strongholds, casting down arguments and every high thing that exalts itself against the knowledge of God, bringing every thought into captivity to the obedience of Christ, and being ready to punish all disobedience when your obedience is fulfilled. **2 CORINTHIANS 10:4–6 NKJV**

I pray that God will make you ready to obey him and that you will always be eager to do right. May Jesus help you do what pleases God. To Jesus Christ be glory forever and ever! Amen. **HEBREWS 13:21 CEV**

Patience

(the ability to wait or endure calmly and without complaint; refusing to be provoked)

The LORD is merciful! He is kind and patient, and his love never fails. **PSALM 103:8 CEV**

So he prayed: Our LORD, I knew from the very beginning that you wouldn't destroy Nineveh. That's why I left my own country and headed for Spain. You are a kind and merciful God, and you are very patient. You always show love, and you don't like to punish anyone, not even foreigners. **JONAH 4:2 CEV**

Don't you see how wonderfully kind, tolerant, and patient God is with you? Does this mean nothing to you? Can't you see that his kindness is intended to turn you from your sin? **ROMANS 2:4 NLT**

For whatever things were written before were written for our learning, that we through the patience and comfort of the Scriptures might have hope. Now may the God of patience and comfort grant you to be like-minded toward one another, according to Christ Jesus. **ROMANS 15:4–5 NKJV**

But the Holy Spirit produces this kind of fruit in our lives: love, joy, peace, patience, kindness, goodness, faithfulness, gentleness, and self-control. There is no law against these things!
GALATIANS 5:22–23 NLT

His glorious power will make you patient and strong enough to endure anything, and you will be truly happy. **COLOSSIANS 1:11 CEV**

Therefore, as God's chosen people, holy and dearly loved, clothe yourselves with compassion, kindness, humility, gentleness and patience. **COLOSSIANS 3:12 NIV**

I pray that the Lord will guide you to be as loving as God and as patient as Christ. **2 THESSALONIANS 3:5 CEV**

But do not forget this one thing, dear friends: With the Lord a day is like a thousand years, and a thousand years are like a day. The Lord is not slow in keeping his promise, as some understand slowness. Instead he is patient with you, not wanting anyone to perish, but everyone to come to repentance . . . Bear in mind that our Lord's patience means salvation. **2 PETER 3:8–9, 15 NIV**

...he is *patient* with you,
not wanting anyone
to perish, but everyone to
come to repentance ...

Peace

(free from conflict; undisturbed)

"For the mountains may be removed and the hills may shake, But My lovingkindness will not be removed from you, And My covenant of peace will not be shaken," Says the Lord who has compassion on you. **ISAIAH 54:10 NASB**

Peace I leave with you; my peace I give you. I do not give to you as the world gives. Do not let your hearts be troubled and do not be afraid. **JOHN 14:27 NIV**

"I have told you these things, so that in me you may have peace. In this world you will have trouble. But take heart! I have overcome the world." **JOHN 16:33 NIV**

There will be trouble and calamity for everyone who keeps on doing what is evil—for the Jew first and also for the Gentile. But there will be glory and honor and peace from God for all who do good—for the Jew first and also for the Gentile. For God does not show favoritism. **ROMANS 2:9–11 NLT**

For the kingdom of God is not a matter of eating and drinking, but of righteousness, peace and joy in the Holy Spirit. **ROMANS 14:17 NIV**

But the fruit of the Spirit is love, joy, peace, forbearance, kindness, goodness, faithfulness, gentleness and self-control. Against such things there is no law. **GALATIANS 5:22–23 NIV**

⁓ continued ⁓

I pray that God the Father and the Lord Jesus Christ will give peace, love, and faith to every follower! EPHESIANS 6:23 CEV

Do not be anxious about anything, but in every situation, by prayer and petition, with thanksgiving, present your requests to God. And the peace of God, which transcends all understanding, will guard your hearts and your minds in Christ Jesus. Finally, brothers and sisters, whatever is true, whatever is noble, whatever is right, whatever is pure, whatever is lovely, whatever is admirable— if anything is excellent or praiseworthy—think about such things. Whatever you have learned or received or heard from me, or seen in me—put it into practice. And the God of peace will be with you. PHILIPPIANS 4:6–9 NIV

Let the peace of Christ rule in your hearts, since as members of one body you were called to peace. And be thankful.
COLOSSIANS 3:15 NIV

Now may the Lord of peace himself give you peace at all times and in every way. The Lord be with all of you. 2 THESSALONIANS 3:16 NIV

Perfection

(complete excellence; without defect; precise; flawless)

God's way is perfect. All the LORD's promises prove true. He is a shield for all who look to him for protection. For who is God except the LORD? Who but our God is a solid rock? God arms me with strength, and he makes my way perfect. He makes me as surefooted as a deer, enabling me to stand on mountain heights. He trains my hands for battle; he strengthens my arm to draw a bronze bow. You have given me your shield of victory. Your right hand supports me; your help has made me great. You have made a wide path for my feet to keep them from slipping. PSALM 18:30–36 NLT

The LORD will perfect *that which* concerns me; Your mercy, O LORD, *endures* forever; Do not forsake the works of Your hands. PSALM 138:8 NKJV

Be perfect, therefore, as your heavenly Father is perfect. MATTHEW 5:48 NIV

Three times I pleaded with the Lord to take it away from me. But he said to me, "My grace is sufficient for you, for my power is made perfect in weakness." Therefore I will boast all the more gladly about my weaknesses, so that Christ's power may rest on me. That is why, for Christ's sake, I delight in weaknesses, in insults, in hardships, in persecutions, in difficulties. For when I am weak, then I am strong. 2 CORINTHIANS 12:8–10 NIV

I don't mean to say that I have already achieved these things or

continued

that I have already reached perfection. But I press on to possess that perfection for which Christ Jesus first possessed me.
PHILIPPIANS 3:12 NLT

Yet now he has reconciled you to himself through the death of Christ in his physical body. As a result, he has brought you into his own presence, and you are holy and blameless as you stand before him without a single fault. COLOSSIANS 1:22 NLT

Epaphras, a member of your own fellowship and a servant of Christ Jesus, sends you his greetings. He always prays earnestly for you, asking God to make you strong and perfect, fully confident that you are following the whole will of God. COLOSSIANS 4:12 NLT

For by that one offering he forever made perfect those who are being made holy. HEBREWS 10:14 NLT

Dear brothers and sisters, when troubles come your way, consider it an opportunity for great joy. For you know that when your faith is tested, your endurance has a chance to grow. So let it grow, for when your endurance is fully developed, you will be perfect and complete, needing nothing. JAMES 1:2–4 NLT

❧ *Day 73* ❧

Power

*(great ability to do, act, produce, influence,
control, or affect)*

And when He had called His twelve disciples to *Him*, He gave them power *over* unclean spirits, to cast them out, and to heal all kinds of sickness and all kinds of disease. MATTHEW 10:1 NKJV

As John grew up, God's Spirit gave him great power. John lived in the desert until the time he was sent to the people of Israel. LUKE 1:80 CEV

And the whole multitude sought to touch Him, for power went out from Him and healed *them* all. LUKE 6:19 NKJV

"But you will receive power when the Holy Spirit comes on you; and you will be my witnesses in Jerusalem, and in all Judea and Samaria, and to the ends of the earth." ACTS 1:8 NIV

God gave Stephen the power to work great miracles and wonders among the people. ACTS 6:8 CEV

When Simon saw that the Spirit was given when the apostles laid their hands on people, he offered them money to buy this power. "Let me have this power, too," he exclaimed, "so that when I lay my hands on people, they will receive the Holy Spirit!" But Peter replied, "May your money be destroyed with you for thinking God's gift can be bought! You can have no part in this, for your heart is not right with God. Repent of your wickedness and pray to the Lord. Perhaps he will forgive your evil thoughts, for I can

see that you are full of bitter jealousy and are held captive by sin."
ACTS 8:18–23 NLT

And my message and my preaching were very plain. Rather than using clever and persuasive speeches, I relied only on the power of the Holy Spirit. I did this so you would trust not in human wisdom but in the power of God. 1 CORINTHIANS 2:4–5 NLT

For the Kingdom of God is not just a lot of talk; it is living by God's power. 1 CORINTHIANS 4:20 NLT

So will it be with the resurrection of the dead. The body that is sown is perishable, it is raised imperishable; it is sown in dishonor, it is raised in glory; it is sown in weakness, it is raised in power; it is sown a natural body, it is raised a spiritual body. If there is a natural body, there is also a spiritual body. 1 CORINTHIANS 15:42–44 NIV

For God has not given us a spirit of fear and timidity, but of power, love, and self-discipline. 2 TIMOTHY 1:7 NLT

Prosperity

(to succeed; to thrive; to have good fortune, wealth, success)

Now his master saw that the LORD was with him and *how* the LORD caused all that he did to prosper in his hand. GENESIS 39:3 NASB

"If I were you, I would go to God and present my case to him. He does great things too marvelous to understand. He performs countless miracles. He gives rain for the earth and water for the fields. He gives prosperity to the poor and protects those who suffer." JOB 5:8–11 NLT

"Submit to God and be at peace with him; in this way prosperity will come to you." JOB 22:21 NIV

How blessed is the man who does not walk in the counsel of the wicked, Nor stand in the way of sinners, Nor sit in the seat of scoffers. But his delight is in the law of the LORD, and in his law he meditates day and night. He will be like a tree *firmly* planted by streams of water, which yields its fruit in its season and its leaf does not wither; And in whatever he does, he prospers. PSALM 1:1–3 NASB

I form the light and create darkness, I bring prosperity and create disaster; I, the LORD, do all these things. ISAIAH 45:7 NIV

And everyone who has left houses or brothers or sisters or father or mother or children or farms for My name's sake, will receive many times as much, and will inherit eternal life. MATTHEW 19:29 NASB

◎∽ continued ∽◎

Let them shout for joy and be glad, Who favor my righteous cause; And let them say continually, "Let the LORD be magnified, Who has pleasure in the prosperity of His servant." And my tongue shall speak of Your righteousness *And* of Your praise all the day long. **PSALM 35:27–28 NKJV**

I want to report to you, friends, that my imprisonment here has had the opposite of its intended effect. Instead of being squelched, the Message has actually prospered. All the soldiers here, and everyone else, too, found out that I'm in jail because of this Messiah. That piqued their curiosity, and now they've learned all about him. Not only that, but most of the followers of Jesus here have become far more sure of themselves in the faith than ever, speaking out fearlessly about God, about the Messiah. **PHILIPPIANS 1:12–14 MSG**

"For I know the plans I have for you," declares the LORD, "plans to prosper you and not to harm you, plans to give you hope and a future." **JEREMIAH 29:11 NIV**

... plans to *prosper you*
and not to harm you,
plans to give you a
hope and a future.

Protection

(to shield from injury, danger, or loss; to defend)

Even though I walk through the darkest valley, I will fear no evil, for you are with me; your rod and your staff, they comfort me. **PSALM 23:4 NIV**

The LORD will keep you from all harm—he will watch over your life; the LORD will watch over your coming and going both now and forevermore. **PSALM 121:7–8 NIV**

The LORD protects all those who love him, but he destroys the wicked. **PSALM 145:20 NLT**

When you pass through the waters, I will be with you; and when you pass through the rivers, they will not sweep over you. When you walk through the fire, you will not be burned; the flames will not set you ablaze. **ISAIAH 43:2 NIV**

I will remain in the world no longer, but they are still in the world, and I am coming to you. Holy Father, protect them by the power of your name, the name you gave me, so that they may be one as we are one. While I was with them, I protected them and kept them safe by that name you gave me. None has been lost except the one doomed to destruction so that Scripture would be fulfilled... My prayer is not that you take them out of the world but that you protect them from the evil one. **JOHN 17:11–12, 15 NIV**

Finally, be strong in the Lord and in his mighty power. Put on the full armor of God, so that you can take your stand against the devil's schemes. For our struggle is not against flesh and blood, but against the rulers, against the authorities, against the powers of this dark world and against the spiritual forces of evil in the heavenly realms. Therefore put on the full armor of God, so that when the day of evil comes, you may be able to stand your ground, and after you have done everything, to stand. Stand firm then, with the belt of truth buckled around your waist, with the breastplate of righteousness in place, and with your feet fitted with the readiness that comes from the gospel of peace. In addition to all this, take up the shield of faith, with which you can extinguish all the flaming arrows of the evil one. Take the helmet of salvation and the sword of the Spirit, which is the word of God. EPHESIANS 6:10–17 NIV

But the Lord is faithful, and he will strengthen you and protect you from the evil one. 2 THESSALONIANS 3:3 NIV

"Because you have obeyed my command to persevere, I will protect you from the great time of testing that will come upon the whole world to test those who belong to this world." REVELATION 3:10 NLT

Provision

*(to supply in order to meet future needs;
to make available)*

Fear the LORD, you his godly people, for those who fear him will
have all they need. Even strong young lions sometimes go hungry,
but those who trust in the LORD will lack no good thing.
PSALM 34:9–10 NLT

O God, when you led your people out from Egypt, when you
marched through the dry wasteland, the earth trembled, and the
heavens poured down rain before you, the God of Sinai, before God,
the God of Israel. You sent abundant rain, O God, to refresh the
weary land. There your people finally settled, and with a bountiful
harvest, O God, you provided for your needy people.
PSALM 68:7–10 NLT

I will bless her with abundant provisions; her poor I will satisfy
with food. PSALM 132:15 NIV

"Therefore I tell you, do not worry about your life, what you will eat
or drink; or about your body, what you will wear. Is not life more
than food, and the body more than clothes? Look at the birds of
the air; they do not sow or reap or store away in barns, and yet your
heavenly Father feeds them. Are you not much more valuable than
they? Can any one of you by worrying add a single hour to your
life? And why do you worry about clothes? See how the flowers
of the field grow. They do not labor or spin. Yet I tell you that not
even Solomon in all his splendor was dressed like one of these. If
that is how God clothes the grass of the field, which is here today

and tomorrow is thrown into the fire, will he not much more clothe you—you of little faith? So do not worry, saying, 'What shall we eat?' or 'What shall we drink?' or 'What shall we wear?' For the pagans run after all these things, and your heavenly Father knows that you need them. But seek first his kingdom and his righteousness, and all these things will be given to you as well. Therefore do not worry about tomorrow, for tomorrow will worry about itself. Each day has enough trouble of its own." MATTHEW 6:25–34 NIV

Give us today our daily bread. MATTHEW 6:11 NIV

"Yet he has not left himself without testimony: He has shown kindness by giving you rain from heaven and crops in their seasons; he provides you with plenty of food and fills your hearts with joy." ACTS 14:17 NIV

At the moment I have all I need—and more! I am generously supplied with the gifts you sent me with Epaphroditus. They are a sweet-smelling sacrifice that is acceptable and pleasing to God. And this same God who takes care of me will supply all your needs from his glorious riches, which have been given to us in Christ Jesus. PHILIPPIANS 4:18–19 NLT

Command those who are rich in this present world not to be arrogant nor to put their hope in wealth, which is so uncertain, but to put their hope in God, who richly provides us with everything for our enjoyment. 1 TIMOTHY 6:17 NIV

Ransom

(to release a captive by paying the demanded price;
to redeem)

Into Your hand I commit my spirit; You have ransomed me,
O LORD, God of truth. PSALM 31:5 NASB

Then I will praise you with music on the harp, because you are
faithful to your promises, O my God. I will sing praises to you
with a lyre, O Holy One of Israel. I will shout for joy and sing your
praises, for you have ransomed me. PSALM 71:22–23 NLT

He has paid a full ransom for his people. He has guaranteed his
covenant with them forever. What a holy, awe-inspiring name he
has! PSALM 111:9 NLT

But now, O Jacob, listen to the LORD who created you. O Israel, the
one who formed you says, "Do not be afraid, for I have ransomed
you. I have called you by name; you are mine. When you go
through deep waters, I will be with you. When you go through
rivers of difficulty, you will not drown. When you walk through the
fire of oppression, you will not be burned up; the flames will not
consume you. For I am the LORD, your God, the Holy One of Israel,
your Savior. I gave Egypt as a ransom for your freedom; I gave
Ethiopia and Seba in your place. Others were given in exchange
for you. I traded their lives for yours because you are precious to
me. You are honored, and I love you." ISAIAH 43:1–4 NLT

For the time has come for me to avenge my people, to ransom them
from their oppressors. I was amazed to see that no one intervened to

help the oppressed. So I myself stepped in to save them with my strong arm, and my wrath sustained me. ISAIAH 63:4–5 NLT

But Jesus called them to *Himself* and said, "You know that the rulers of the Gentiles lord it over them, and those who are great exercise authority over them. Yet it shall not be so among you; but whoever desires to become great among you, let him be your servant. And whoever desires to be first among you, let him be your slave—just as the Son of Man did not come to be served, but to serve, and to give His life a ransom for many." MATTHEW 20:25–28 NKJV

And remember that the heavenly Father to whom you pray has no favorites. He will judge or reward you according to what you do. So you must live in reverent fear of him during your time as "foreigners in the land." For you know that God paid a ransom to save you from the empty life you inherited from your ancestors. And the ransom he paid was not mere gold or silver. It was the precious blood of Christ, the sinless, spotless Lamb of God. God chose him as your ransom long before the world began, but he has now revealed him to you in these last days. 1 PETER 1:17–20 NLT

Reconciliation

(to settle a dispute; to bring into harmony)

You see, at just the right time, when we were still powerless, Christ died for the ungodly. Very rarely will anyone die for a righteous person, though for a good person someone might possibly dare to die. But God demonstrates his own love for us in this: While we were still sinners, Christ died for us. Since we have now been justified by his blood, how much more shall we be saved from God's wrath through him! For if, while we were God's enemies, we were reconciled to him through the death of his Son, how much more, having been reconciled, shall we be saved through his life! Not only is this so, but we also boast in God through our Lord Jesus Christ, through whom we have now received reconciliation.
ROMANS 5:6–11 NIV

So from now on we regard no one from a worldly point of view. Though we once regarded Christ in this way, we do so no longer. Therefore, if anyone is in Christ, the new creation has come: The old has gone, the new is here! All this is from God, who reconciled us to himself through Christ and gave us the ministry of reconciliation: that God was reconciling the world to himself in Christ, not counting people's sins against them. And he has committed to us the message of reconciliation. We are therefore Christ's ambassadors, as though God were making his appeal through us. We implore you on Christ's behalf: Be reconciled to God. God made him who had no sin to be sin for us, so that in him we might become the righteousness of God.
2 CORINTHIANS 5:16–21 NIV

For Christ himself has brought peace to us. He united Jews and Gentiles into one people when, in his own body on the cross, he broke down the wall of hostility that separated us. He did this by ending the system of law with its commandments and regulations. He made peace between Jews and Gentiles by creating in himself one new people from the two groups. Together as one body, Christ reconciled both groups to God by means of his death on the cross, and our hostility toward each other was put to death. He brought this Good News of peace to you Gentiles who were far away from him, and peace to the Jews who were near. Now all of us can come to the Father through the same Holy Spirit because of what Christ has done for us. EPHESIANS 2:14–18 NLT

For God in all his fullness was pleased to live in Christ, and through him God reconciled everything to himself. He made peace with everything in heaven and on earth by means of Christ's blood on the cross. This includes you who were once far away from God. You were his enemies, separated from him by your evil thoughts and actions. Yet now he has reconciled you to himself through the death of Christ in his physical body. As a result, he has brought you into his own presence, and you are holy and blameless as you stand before him without a single fault. COLOSSIANS 1:19–22 NLT

For there is only one God and one Mediator who can reconcile God and humanity—the man Christ Jesus. 1 TIMOTHY 2:5 NLT

Redemption

(to deliver from sin and its penalties; to make amends for; to restore to favor)

He provided redemption for his people; he ordained his covenant forever—holy and awesome is his name. **PSALM 111:9 NIV**

Israel, put your hope in the LORD, for with the LORD is unfailing love and with him is full redemption. He himself will redeem Israel from all their sins. **PSALM 130:7–8 NIV**

But now, this is what the LORD says—he who created you, Jacob, he who formed you, Israel: "Do not fear, for I have redeemed you; I have summoned you by name; you are mine." **ISAIAH 43:1 NIV**

"Praise be to the Lord, the God of Israel, because he has come to his people and redeemed them." **LUKE 1:68 NIV**

Praise be to the God and Father of our Lord Jesus Christ, who has blessed us in the heavenly realms with every spiritual blessing in Christ. For he chose us in him before the creation of the world to be holy and blameless in his sight. In love he predestined us for adoption to sonship through Jesus Christ, in accordance with his pleasure and will—to the praise of his glorious grace, which he has freely given us in the One he loves. In him we have redemption through his blood, the forgiveness of sins, in accordance with the riches of God's grace that he lavished on us. With all wisdom and understanding, he made known to us the mystery of his will according to his good pleasure, which he purposed in Christ, to be put into effect when the times reach their fulfillment—

to bring unity to all things in heaven and on earth under Christ. In him we were also chosen, having been predestined according to the plan of him who works out everything in conformity with the purpose of his will, in order that we, who were the first to put our hope in Christ, might be for the praise of his glory. And you also were included in Christ when you heard the message of truth, the gospel of your salvation. When you believed, you were marked in him with a seal, the promised Holy Spirit, who is a deposit guaranteeing our inheritance until the redemption of those who are God's possession—to the praise of his glory. EPHESIANS 1:3–14 NIV

For he has rescued us from the dominion of darkness and brought us into the kingdom of the Son he loves, in whom we have redemption, the forgiveness of sins. COLOSSIANS 1:13–14 NIV

...we have *redemption*,
the *forgiveness* of sins.

Refuge

(a place of safety; shelter; a safe retreat)

David sang to the LORD the words of this song when the LORD delivered him from the hand of all his enemies and from the hand of Saul. He said: "The LORD is my rock, my fortress and my deliverer; my God is my rock, in whom I take refuge, my shield and the horn of my salvation. He is my stronghold, my refuge and my savior—from violent people you save me. I called to the LORD, who is worthy of praise, and have been saved from my enemies ... As for God, his way is perfect: The LORD's word is flawless; he shields all who take refuge in him. For who is God besides the LORD? And who is the Rock except our God? It is God who arms me with strength and keeps my way secure."
2 SAMUEL 22:1–4, 31–33 NIV

But let all who take refuge in you be glad; let them ever sing for joy. Spread your protection over them, that those who love your name may rejoice in you. PSALM 5:11 NIV

The LORD also will be a refuge for the oppressed, A refuge in times of trouble. PSALM 9:9 NKJV

The LORD is my rock, my fortress and my deliverer; my God is my rock, in whom I take refuge, my shield and the horn of my salvation, my stronghold. PSALM 18:2 NIV

O taste and see that the LORD is good; How blessed is the man who takes refuge in Him! ... The LORD redeems the soul of His servants,

And none of those who take refuge in Him will be condemned.
PSALM 34:8, 22 NASB

God is our refuge and strength, an ever-present help in trouble.
PSALM 46:1 NIV

Have mercy on me, my God, have mercy on me, for in you I take refuge. I will take refuge in the shadow of your wings until the disaster has passed. **PSALM 57:1 NIV**

The LORD will roar from Zion and thunder from Jerusalem; the earth and the heavens will tremble. But the LORD will be a refuge for his people, a stronghold for the people of Israel. **JOEL 3:16 NIV**

The LORD is good, a refuge in times of trouble. He cares for those who trust in him . . . **NAHUM 1:7 NIV**

The LORD is *good,*
a *refuge* in times
of trouble.

Renewal

(to give new spiritual strength; to make new or new again; to refill with a fresh supply)

The LORD is my shepherd; I have all that I need. He lets me rest in green meadows; he leads me beside peaceful streams. He renews my strength. He guides me along right paths, bringing honor to his name. PSALM 23:1–3 NLT

Create in me a clean heart, O God. Renew a loyal spirit within me. PSALM 51:10 NLT

I cried out, "I am slipping!" but your unfailing love, O LORD, supported me. When doubts filled my mind, your comfort gave me renewed hope and cheer. PSALM 94:18–19 NLT

The LORD will extend your powerful kingdom from Jerusalem; you will rule over your enemies. When you go to war, your people will serve you willingly. You are arrayed in holy garments, and your strength will be renewed each day like the morning dew. PSALM 110:2–3 NLT

He gives power to the weak, And to those who have no might He increases strength. Even the youths shall faint and be weary, And the young men shall utterly fall, But those who wait on the LORD Shall renew *their* strength; They shall mount up with wings like eagles, They shall run and not be weary, They shall walk and not faint. ISAIAH 40:29–31 NKJV

Repent, then, and turn to God, so that your sins may be wiped out, that times of refreshing may come from the Lord . . . **ACTS 3:19 NIV**

Do not conform to the pattern of this world, but be transformed by the renewing of your mind. Then you will be able to test and approve what God's will is—his good, pleasing and perfect will. **ROMANS 12:2 NIV**

Put on your new nature, and be renewed as you learn to know your Creator and become like him. In this new life, it doesn't matter if you are a Jew or a Gentile, circumcised or uncircumcised, barbaric, uncivilized, slave, or free. Christ is all that matters, and he lives in all of us. **COLOSSIANS 3:10–11 NLT**

At one time we too were foolish, disobedient, deceived and enslaved by all kinds of passions and pleasures. We lived in malice and envy, being hated and hating one another. But when the kindness and love of God our Savior appeared, he saved us, not because of righteous things we had done, but because of his mercy. He saved us through the washing of rebirth and renewal by the Holy Spirit, whom he poured out on us generously through Jesus Christ our Savior, so that, having been justified by his grace, we might become heirs having the hope of eternal life. **TITUS 3:3–7 NIV**

Rescue

*(to free or save from imminent danger,
imprisonment, or evil)*

Pray like this: Our Father in heaven, may your name be kept holy. May your Kingdom come soon. May your will be done on earth, as it is in heaven. Give us today the food we need, and forgive us our sins, as we have forgiven those who sin against us. And don't let us yield to temptation, but rescue us from the evil one. **MATTHEW 6:9–13 NLT**

We have been rescued from our enemies so we can serve God without fear, in holiness and righteousness for as long as we live. **LUKE 1:74–75 NLT**

It's news I'm most proud to proclaim, this extraordinary Message of God's powerful plan to rescue everyone who trusts him, starting with Jews and then right on to everyone else! God's way of putting people right shows up in the acts of faith, confirming what Scripture has said all along: "The person in right standing before God by trusting him really lives." **ROMANS 1:16–17 MSG**

We don't want you in the dark, friends, about how hard it was when all this came down on us in Asia province. It was so bad we didn't think we were going to make it. We felt like we'd been sent to death row, that it was all over for us. As it turned out, it was the best thing that could have happened. Instead of trusting in our own strength or wits to get out of it, we were forced to trust God totally—not a bad idea since he's the God who raises the dead! And he did it, rescued us from certain doom. *And* he'll do it again, rescuing us as many times as we need rescuing. You and your prayers are part of the rescue operation—I don't want you in the dark about that either. I can see your faces even now, lifted in praise for God's deliverance of us, a rescue in which your prayers played such a crucial part. **2 CORINTHIANS 1:8–11 MSG**

Jesus gave his life for our sins, just as God our Father planned, in order to rescue us from this evil world in which we live.
GALATIANS 1:4 NLT

We also pray that you will be strengthened with all his glorious power so you will have all the endurance and patience you need. May you be filled with joy, always thanking the Father. He has enabled you to share in the inheritance that belongs to his people, who live in the light. For he has rescued us from the kingdom of darkness and transferred us into the Kingdom of his dear Son, who purchased our freedom and forgave our sins.
COLOSSIANS 1:11–14 NLT

For he has *rescued*
us from the
kingdom of darkness…

Rest

*(supernatural peace, ease, or calm;
tranquility of mind; relief)*

"Praise be to the LORD, who has given rest to his people Israel just
as he promised. Not one word has failed of all the good promises
he gave through his servant Moses." 1 KINGS 8:56 NIV

The LORD is my shepherd; I have all that I need. He lets me rest in
green meadows; he leads me beside peaceful streams.
PSALM 23:1–2 NLT

Truly my soul finds rest in God; my salvation comes from him . . .
Yes, my soul, find rest in God; my hope comes from him.
PSALM 62:1, 5 NIV

Unless the LORD builds a house, the work of the builders is wasted.
Unless the LORD protects a city, guarding it with sentries will do
no good. It is useless for you to work so hard from early morning
until late at night, anxiously working for food to eat; for God gives
rest to his loved ones. PSALM 127:1–2 NLT

"Come to me, all you who are weary and burdened, and I will give
you rest. Take my yoke upon you and learn from me, for I am gentle
and humble in heart, and you will find rest for your souls. For my
yoke is easy and my burden is light." MATTHEW 11:28–30 NIV

God's promise of entering his rest still stands, so we ought to
tremble with fear that some of you might fail to experience
it. For this good news—that God has prepared this rest—has been

announced to us just as it was to them. But it did them no good because they didn't share the faith of those who listened to God. For only we who believe can enter his rest. As for the others, God said, "In my anger I took an oath: 'They will never enter my place of rest,'" even though this rest has been ready since he made the world. We know it is ready because of the place in the Scriptures where it mentions the seventh day: "On the seventh day God rested from all his work." But in the other passage God said, "They will never enter my place of rest." So God's rest is there for people to enter, but those who first heard this good news failed to enter because they disobeyed God. So God set another time for entering his rest, and that time is today. God announced this through David much later in the words already quoted: "Today when you hear his voice, don't harden your hearts." Now if Joshua had succeeded in giving them this rest, God would not have spoken about another day of rest still to come. So there is a special rest still waiting for the people of God. For all who have entered into God's rest have rested from their labors, just as God did after creating the world. So let us do our best to enter that rest. But if we disobey God, as the people of Israel did, we will fall. HEBREWS 4:1–11 NLT

Restoration

(reinstate; restitution for loss; bringing back to a former, unimpaired state)

When all these blessings and curses I have set before you come on you and you take them to heart wherever the LORD your God disperses you among the nations, and when you and your children return to the LORD your God and obey him with all your heart and with all your soul according to everything I command you today, then the LORD your God will restore your fortunes and have compassion on you and gather you again from all the nations where he scattered you. Even if you have been banished to the most distant land under the heavens, from there the LORD your God will gather you and bring you back. He will bring you to the land that belonged to your ancestors, and you will take possession of it. He will make you more prosperous and numerous than your ancestors. DEUTERONOMY 30:1–5 NIV

Your righteousness, O God, reaches to the highest heavens. You have done such wonderful things. Who can compare with you, O God? You have allowed me to suffer much hardship, but you will restore me to life again and lift me up from the depths of the earth. You will restore me to even greater honor and comfort me once again. Then I will praise you with music on the harp, because you are faithful to your promises, O my God. I will sing praises to you with a lyre, O Holy One of Israel. PSALM 71:19–22 NLT

Restore our fortunes, LORD, as streams renew the desert. PSALM 126:4 NLT

Return to your fortress, you prisoners of hope; even now I announce that I will restore twice as much to you. ZECHARIAH 9:12 NIV

Departing from there, Jesus went along by the Sea of Galilee, and having gone up on the mountain, He was sitting there. And large crowds came to Him, bringing with them *those who were* lame, crippled, blind, mute, and many others, and they laid them down at His feet; and He healed them. So the crowd marveled as they saw the mute speaking, the crippled restored, and the lame walking, and the blind seeing; and they glorified the God of Israel. MATTHEW 15:29–31 NASB

Now repent of your sins and turn to God, so that your sins may be wiped away. Then times of refreshment will come from the presence of the Lord, and he will again send you Jesus, your appointed Messiah. For he must remain in heaven until the time for the final restoration of all things, as God promised long ago through his holy prophets. ACTS 3:19–21 NLT

In his kindness God called you to share in his eternal glory by means of Christ Jesus. So after you have suffered a little while, he will restore, support, and strengthen you, and he will place you on a firm foundation. 1 PETER 5:10 NLT

Revelation

*(God's manifestation to humanity of himself or of his will;
communication of divine truth)*

"But don't be afraid of those who threaten you. For the time is coming when everything that is covered will be revealed, and all that is secret will be made known to all. What I tell you now in the darkness, shout abroad when daybreak comes. What I whisper in your ear, shout from the housetops for all to hear!"
MATTHEW 10:26–27 NLT

At that time Jesus said, "I praise you, Father, Lord of heaven and earth, because you have hidden these things from the wise and learned, and revealed them to little children. Yes, Father, for this is what you were pleased to do. All things have been committed to me by my Father. No one knows the Son except the Father, and no one knows the Father except the Son and those to whom the Son chooses to reveal him." MATTHEW 11:25–27 NIV

He did not say anything to them without using a parable. But when he was alone with his own disciples, he explained everything.
MARK 4:34 NIV

No one has ever seen God. But the unique One, who is himself God, is near to the Father's heart. He has revealed God to us.
JOHN 1:18 NLT

Jesus told him, "I am the way, the truth, and the life. No one can come to the Father except through me. If you had really known me, you would know who my Father is. From now on, you do know

him and have seen him!" JOHN 14:6–7 NLT

Surely you have heard about the administration of God's grace that was given to me for you, that is, the mystery made known to me by revelation, as I have already written briefly. In reading this, then, you will be able to understand my insight into the mystery of Christ, which was not made known to people in other generations as it has now been revealed by the Spirit to God's holy apostles and prophets. This mystery is that through the gospel the Gentiles are heirs together with Israel, members together of one body, and sharers together in the promise in Christ Jesus. EPHESIANS 3:2–6 NIV

Without question, this is the great mystery of our faith: Christ was revealed in a human body and vindicated by the Spirit. He was seen by angels and announced to the nations. He was believed in throughout the world and taken to heaven in glory.
1 TIMOTHY 3:16 NLT

Christ was revealed
in a *human body* and
vindicated by the *Spirit*.

Reward

(something given in return for good or evil or merit; compensation)

Whoever is kind to the poor lends to the LORD, and he will reward them for what they have done. PROVERBS 19:17 NIV

If your enemy is hungry, give him food to eat; if he is thirsty, give him water to drink. In doing this, you will heap burning coals on his head, and the LORD will reward you. PROVERBS 25:21-22 NIV

Tell the godly that all will be well for them. They will enjoy the rich reward they have earned! ISAIAH 3:10 NLT

"Blessed are you when people insult you, persecute you and falsely say all kinds of evil against you because of me. Rejoice and be glad, because great is your reward in heaven, for in the same way they persecuted the prophets who were before you."
MATTHEW 5:11-12 NIV

"Be careful not to practice your righteousness in front of others to be seen by them. If you do, you will have no reward from your Father in heaven. So when you give to the needy, do not announce it with trumpets, as the hypocrites do in the synagogues and on the streets, to be honored by others. Truly I tell you, they have received their reward in full. But when you give to the needy, do not let your left hand know what your right hand is doing, so that your giving may be in secret. Then your Father, who sees what is done in secret, will reward you. And when you pray, do not be like the hypocrites, for they love to pray standing in the synagogues

and on the street corners to be seen by others. Truly I tell you, they have received their reward in full. But when you pray, go into your room, close the door and pray to your Father, who is unseen. Then your Father, who sees what is done in secret, will reward you." . . . "When you fast, do not look somber as the hypocrites do, for they disfigure their faces to show others they are fasting. Truly I tell you, they have received their reward in full. But when you fast, put oil on your head and wash your face, so that it will not be obvious to others that you are fasting, but only to your Father, who is unseen; and your Father, who sees what is done in secret, will reward you."
MATTHEW 6:1–6, 16–18 NIV

"Anyone who welcomes you welcomes me, and anyone who welcomes me welcomes the one who sent me. Whoever welcomes a prophet as a prophet will receive a prophet's reward, and whoever welcomes a righteous person as a righteous person will receive a righteous person's reward. And if anyone gives even a cup of cold water to one of these little ones who is my disciple, truly I tell you, that person will certainly not lose their reward."
MATTHEW 10:40–42 NIV

Righteousness

(morally right; morally justifiable; having right standing with God)

For it is not those who hear the law who are righteous in God's sight, but it is those who obey the law who will be declared righteous.
ROMANS 2:13 NIV

But now apart from the law the righteousness of God has been made known, to which the Law and the Prophets testify. This righteousness is given through faith in Jesus Christ to all who believe. There is no difference between Jew and Gentile, for all have sinned and fall short of the glory of God, and all are justified freely by his grace through the redemption that came by Christ Jesus. God presented Christ as a sacrifice of atonement, through the shedding of his blood—to be received by faith. He did this to demonstrate his righteousness, because in his forbearance he had left the sins committed beforehand unpunished—he did it to demonstrate his righteousness at the present time, so as to be just and the one who justifies those who have faith in Jesus.
ROMANS 3:21–26 NIV

And since we have been made right in God's sight by the blood of Christ, he will certainly save us from God's condemnation.
ROMANS 5:9 NLT

God made him who had no sin to be sin for us, so that in him we might become the righteousness of God. 2 CORINTHIANS 5:21 NIV

"I have been crucified with Christ and I no longer live, but Christ lives in me. The life I now live in the body, I live by faith in the Son of God, who loved me and gave himself for me. I do not set aside the grace of God, for if righteousness could be gained through the law, Christ died for nothing!" **GALATIANS 2:20–21 NIV**

And this is my prayer: that your love may abound more and more in knowledge and depth of insight, so that you may be able to discern what is best and may be pure and blameless for the day of Christ, filled with the fruit of righteousness that comes through Jesus Christ—to the glory and praise of God. **PHILIPPIANS 1:9–11 NIV**

"Because of his grace he declared us righteous and gave us confidence that we will inherit eternal life." **TITUS 3:7 NLT**

And He Himself bore our sins in His body on the cross, so that we might die to sin and live to righteousness; for by His wounds you were healed. **1 PETER 2:24 NASB**

Since we know that Christ is righteous, we also know that all who do what is right are God's children. **1 JOHN 2:29 NLT**

Sacrifice

(the act of offering one life for another to honor God)

"I am the good shepherd. The good shepherd sacrifices his life for the sheep. A hired hand will run when he sees a wolf coming. He will abandon the sheep because they don't belong to him and he isn't their shepherd. And so the wolf attacks them and scatters the flock. The hired hand runs away because he's working only for the money and doesn't really care about the sheep. I am the good shepherd; I know my own sheep, and they know me, just as my Father knows me and I know the Father. So I sacrifice my life for the sheep. I have other sheep, too, that are not in this sheepfold. I must bring them also. They will listen to my voice, and there will be one flock with one shepherd. The Father loves me because I sacrifice my life so I may take it back again. No one can take my life from me. I sacrifice it voluntarily. For I have the authority to lay it down when I want to and also to take it up again. For this is what my Father has commanded." JOHN 10:11–18 NLT

And I give myself as a holy sacrifice for them so they can be made holy by your truth. JOHN 17:19 NLT

For God presented Jesus as the sacrifice for sin. People are made right with God when they believe that Jesus sacrificed his life, shedding his blood. This sacrifice shows that God was being fair when he held back and did not punish those who sinned in times past . . . ROMANS 3:25 NLT

The law of Moses was unable to save us because of the weakness of our sinful nature. So God did what the law could not do. He sent his own Son in a body like the bodies we sinners have. And in that body God declared an end to sin's control over us by giving his Son as a sacrifice for our sins. ROMANS 8:3 NLT

Follow God's example, therefore, as dearly loved children and walk in the way of love, just as Christ loved us and gave himself up for us as a fragrant offering and sacrifice to God. EPHESIANS 5:1–2 NIV

Unlike those other high priests, he does not need to offer sacrifices every day. They did this for their own sins first and then for the sins of the people. But Jesus did this once for all when he offered himself as the sacrifice for the people's sins. HEBREWS 7:27 NLT

For by the power of the eternal Spirit, Christ offered himself to God as a perfect sacrifice for our sins. HEBREWS 9:14 NLT

And just as each person is destined to die once and after that comes judgment, so also Christ died once for all time as a sacrifice to take away the sins of many people. He will come again, not to deal with our sins, but to bring salvation to all who are eagerly waiting for him. HEBREWS 9:27–28 NLT

He is the atoning sacrifice for our sins, and not only for ours but also for the sins of the whole world. 1 JOHN 2:2 NIV

This is real love—not that we loved God, but that he loved us and sent his Son as a sacrifice to take away our sins. 1 JOHN 4:10 NLT

Salvation

(to save; deliverance from sin and the penalty of sin)

"She will give birth to a son, and you are to give him the name Jesus, because he will save his people from their sins." **MATTHEW 1:21 NIV**

Whoever believes and is baptized will be saved, but whoever does not believe will be condemned. **MARK 16:16 NIV**

For unto you is born this day in the city of David a Savior, who is Christ the Lord. **LUKE 2:11 ESV**

"For God so loved the world, that He gave His only begotten Son, that whoever believes in Him shall not perish, but have eternal life. For God did not send the Son into the world to judge the world, but that the world might be saved through Him." **JOHN 3:16–17 NASB**

Then said Jesus unto them again, Verily, verily, I say unto you, I am the door of the sheep. All that ever came before me are thieves and robbers: but the sheep did not hear them. I am the door: by me if any man enter in, he shall be saved, and shall go in and out, and find pasture. The thief cometh not, but for to steal, and to kill, and to destroy: I am come that they might have life, and that they might have it more abundantly. I am the good shepherd: the good shepherd giveth his life for the sheep. **JOHN 10:7–11 KJV**

While Jesus was here on earth, he offered prayers and pleadings, with a loud cry and tears, to the one who could rescue him from death. And God heard his prayers because of his deep reverence for God. Even though Jesus was God's Son, he learned obedience from the things he suffered. In this way, God qualified him as a perfect High Priest, and he became the source of eternal salvation for all those who obey him. And God designated him to be a High Priest in the order of Melchizedek. HEBREWS 5:7–10 NLT

Jesus is "'the stone you builders rejected, which has become the cornerstone.' Salvation is found in no one else, for there is no other name under heaven given to mankind by which we must be saved." ACTS 4:11–12 NIV

God saved you by his grace when you believed. And you can't take credit for this; it is a gift from God. Salvation is not a reward for the good things we have done, so none of us can boast about it. EPHESIANS 2:8–9 NLT

God saved you
by his grace when
you believed.

Sanctification

(to purify; to set apart as holy)

My prayer is not that you take them out of the world but that you
protect them from the evil one. They are not of the world, even as
I am not of it. Sanctify them by the truth; your word is truth. As you
sent me into the world, I have sent them into the world. For them
I sanctify myself, that they too may be truly sanctified.
JOHN 17:15–19 NIV

But thanks be to God that though you were slaves of sin, you
became obedient from the heart to that form of teaching to
which you were committed, and having been freed from sin, you
became slaves of righteousness. I am speaking in human terms
because of the weakness of your flesh. For just as you presented
your members as slaves to impurity and to lawlessness, resulting
in *further* lawlessness, so now present your members as slaves
to righteousness, resulting in sanctification. For when you were
slaves of sin, you were free in regard to righteousness. Therefore
what benefit were you then deriving from the things of which you
are now ashamed? For the outcome of those things is death. But
now having been freed from sin and enslaved to God, you derive
your benefit, resulting in sanctification, and the outcome, eternal
life. For the wages of sin is death, but the free gift of God is eternal
life in Christ Jesus our Lord. **ROMANS 6:17–23 NASB**

But you were washed, you were sanctified, you were justified in
the name of the Lord Jesus Christ and by the Spirit of our God.
1 CORINTHIANS 6:11 NIV

But by His doing you are in Christ Jesus, who became to us wisdom from God, and righteousness and sanctification, and redemption, so that, just as it is written, "LET HIM WHO BOASTS, BOAST IN THE LORD." 1 CORINTHIANS 1:30–31 NASB

Now may the God of peace Himself sanctify you completely; and may your whole spirit, soul, and body be preserved blameless at the coming of our Lord Jesus Christ. 1 THESSALONIANS 5:23 NKJV

But we ought always to thank God for you, brothers and sisters loved by the Lord, because God chose you as first fruits to be saved through the sanctifying work of the Spirit and through belief in the truth. 2 THESSALONIANS 2:13 NIV

For both He who sanctifies and those who are sanctified are all from one *Father*; for which reason He is not ashamed to call them brethren . . . HEBREWS 2:11 NASB

For by one offering He has perfected forever those who are being sanctified. HEBREWS 10:14 NKJV

Security

(free from fear, anxiety, worry, or danger)

Bring to an end the violence of the wicked and make the righteous secure—you, the righteous God who probes minds and hearts. PSALM 7:9 NIV

It is God who arms me with strength and keeps my way secure. PSALM 18:32 NIV

When I felt my feet slipping, you came with your love and kept me steady. And when I was burdened with worries, you comforted me and made me feel secure. PSALM 94:18–19 CEV

But I cried to him, "O my God, who lives forever, don't take my life while I am so young! Long ago you laid the foundation of the earth and made the heavens with your hands. They will perish, but you remain forever; they will wear out like old clothing. You will change them like a garment and discard them. But you are always the same; you will live forever. The children of your people will live in security. Their children's children will thrive in your presence." PSALM 102:24–28 NLT

"But he who listens to me shall live securely And will be at ease from the dread of evil." PROVERBS 1:33 NASB

You can go to bed without fear; you will lie down and sleep soundly. You need not be afraid of sudden disaster or the destruction that comes upon the wicked, for the LORD is your security. He will keep your foot from being caught in a trap. **PROVERBS 3:24–26 NLT**

Whoever fears the LORD has a secure fortress, and for their children it will be a refuge … When calamity comes, the wicked are brought down, but even in death the righteous seek refuge in God. **PROVERBS 14:26, 32 NIV**

"Like a swallow, *like* a crane, so I twitter; I moan like a dove; My eyes look wistfully to the heights; O LORD, I am oppressed, be my security." **ISAIAH 38:14 NASB**

We know that God's children do not make a practice of sinning, for God's Son holds them securely, and the evil one cannot touch them. **1 JOHN 5:18 NLT**

…God's Son holds them securely, and *the evil one* cannot touch them.

Self-control

(control of one's emotions, desires, actions)

But the fruit of the Spirit is love, joy, peace, forbearance, kindness, goodness, faithfulness, gentleness and self-control. Against such things there is no law. Those who belong to Christ Jesus have crucified the flesh with its passions and desires.
GALATIANS 5:22–24 NIV

God's Spirit doesn't make cowards out of us. The Spirit gives us power, love, and self-control. **2 TIMOTHY 1:7 CEV**

For the grace of God has appeared that offers salvation to all people. It teaches us to say "No" to ungodliness and worldly passions, and to live self-controlled, upright and godly lives in this present age, while we wait for the blessed hope—the appearing of the glory of our great God and Savior, Jesus Christ, who gave himself for us to redeem us from all wickedness and to purify for himself a people that are his very own, eager to do what is good.
TITUS 2:11–14 NIV

His divine power has given us everything we need for a godly life through our knowledge of him who called us by his own glory and goodness. Through these he has given us his very great and precious promises, so that through them you may participate in the divine nature, having escaped the corruption in the world caused by evil desires. For this very reason, make every effort to add to your faith goodness; and to goodness, knowledge; and to knowledge, self-control; and to self-control, perseverance; and

to perseverance, godliness; and to godliness, mutual affection; and to mutual affection, love. For if you possess these qualities in increasing measure, they will keep you from being ineffective and unproductive in your knowledge of our Lord Jesus Christ.
2 PETER 1:3–8 NIV

His *divine power* has given us everything we need for a godly life *through our knowledge of him* who called us by his own *glory and goodness.*

Spiritual Gifts

*(supernatural gift imparted by the Holy Spirit
after receiving Christ)*

For just as each of us has one body with many members, and these members do not all have the same function, so in Christ we, though many, form one body, and each member belongs to all the others. We have different gifts, according to the grace given to each of us. If your gift is prophesying, then prophesy in accordance with your faith; if it is serving, then serve; if it is teaching, then teach; if it is to encourage, then give encouragement; if it is giving, then give generously; if it is to lead, do it diligently; if it is to show mercy, do it cheerfully. ROMANS 12:4–8 NIV

There are different kinds of gifts, but the same Spirit distributes them. There are different kinds of service, but the same LORD. There are different kinds of working, but in all of them and in everyone it is the same God at work. Now to each one the manifestation of the Spirit is given for the common good. To one there is given through the Spirit a message of wisdom, to another a message of knowledge by means of the same Spirit, to another faith by the same Spirit, to another gifts of healing by that one Spirit, to another miraculous powers, to another prophecy, to another distinguishing between spirits, to another speaking in different kinds of tongues, and to still another the interpretation of tongues. All these are the work of one and the same Spirit, and he distributes them to each one, just as he determines. 1 CORINTHIANS 12:4–11 NIV

For there is one body and one Spirit, just as you have been called to one glorious hope for the future. There is one Lord, one faith, one baptism, and one God and Father, who is over all and in all and living through all. However, he has given each one of us a special gift through the generosity of Christ. That is why the Scriptures say, "When he ascended to the heights, he led a crowd of captives and gave gifts to his people." . . . Now these are the gifts Christ gave to the church: the apostles, the prophets, the evangelists, and the pastors and teachers. Their responsibility is to equip God's people to do his work and build up the church, the body of Christ. This will continue until we all come to such unity in our faith and knowledge of God's Son that we will be mature in the Lord, measuring up to the full and complete standard of Christ. Then we will no longer be immature like children. We won't be tossed and blown about by every wind of new teaching. We will not be influenced when people try to trick us with lies so clever they sound like the truth. Instead, we will speak the truth in love, growing in every way more and more like Christ, who is the head of his body, the church. He makes the whole body fit together perfectly. As each part does its own special work, it helps the other parts grow, so that the whole body is healthy and growing and full of love. EPHESIANS 4:4–8, 11–16 NLT

And God confirmed the message by giving signs and wonders and various miracles and gifts of the Holy Spirit whenever he chose. HEBREWS 2:4 NLT

God has given each of you a gift from his great variety of spiritual gifts. Use them well to serve one another. Do you have the gift of speaking? Then speak as though God himself were speaking through you. Do you have the gift of helping others? Do it with all the strength and energy that God supplies. Then everything you do will bring glory to God through Jesus Christ. All glory and power to him forever and ever! Amen. 1 PETER 4:10–11 NLT

Strength

(strong; durable; the power to resist)

The eyes of the LORD search the whole earth in order to strengthen those whose hearts are fully committed to him.
2 CHRONICLES 16:9 NLT

God is our refuge and strength, always ready to help in times of trouble. **PSALM 46:1 NLT**

My health may fail, and my spirit may grow weak, but God remains the strength of my heart; he is mine forever. **PSALM 73:26 NLT**

He gives power to the weak and strength to the powerless.
ISAIAH 40:29 NLT

And on the basis of faith in His name, *it is* the name of Jesus which has strengthened this man whom you see and know; and the faith which *comes* through Him has given him this perfect health in the presence of you all. **ACTS 3:16 NASB**

Then the church throughout Judea, Galilee and Samaria enjoyed a time of peace and was strengthened. Living in the fear of the Lord and encouraged by the Holy Spirit, it increased in numbers.
ACTS 9:31 NIV

He will keep you strong to the end so that you will be free from all blame on the day when our Lord Jesus Christ returns.
1 CORINTHIANS 1:8 NLT

It is the same way with the resurrection of the dead. Our earthly bodies are planted in the ground when we die, but they will be raised to live forever. Our bodies are buried in brokenness, but they will be raised in glory. They are buried in weakness, but they will be raised in strength. 1 CORINTHIANS 15:42–43 NLT

And He said to me, "My grace is sufficient for you, for My strength is made perfect in weakness." Therefore most gladly I will rather boast in my infirmities, that the power of Christ may rest upon me. 2 CORINTHIANS 12:9 NKJV

I pray that from his glorious, unlimited resources he will empower you with inner strength through his Spirit. Then Christ will make his home in your hearts as you trust in him. Your roots will grow down into God's love and keep you strong. EPHESIANS 3:16–17 NLT

For I can do everything through Christ, who gives me strength. PHILIPPIANS 4:13 NLT

But the Lord is faithful, and He will strengthen and protect you from the evil one. 2 THESSALONIANS 3:3 NASB

So never be ashamed to tell others about our Lord. And don't be ashamed of me, either, even though I'm in prison for him. With the strength God gives you, be ready to suffer with me for the sake of the Good News. 2 TIMOTHY 1:8 NLT

Truth

(the quality of being genuine or factual)

The Word became flesh and made his dwelling among us. We have seen his glory, the glory of the one and only Son, who came from the Father, full of grace and truth . . . For the law was given through Moses; grace and truth came through Jesus Christ.
JOHN 1:14, 17 NIV

"The One who comes from above is head and shoulders over other messengers from God. The earthborn is earthbound and speaks earth language; the heavenborn is in a league of his own. He sets out the evidence of what he saw and heard in heaven. No one wants to deal with these facts. But anyone who examines this evidence will come to stake his life on this: that God himself is the truth." JOHN 3:31–33 MSG

But an hour is coming, and now is, when the true worshipers will worship the Father in spirit and truth; for such people the Father seeks to be His worshipers. JOHN 4:23 NASB

To the Jews who had believed him, Jesus said, "If you hold to my teaching, you are really my disciples. Then you will know the truth, and the truth will set you free." JOHN 8:31–32 NIV

Jesus answered, "I am the way and the truth and the life. No one comes to the Father except through me." JOHN 14:6 NIV

"You are a king, then!" said Pilate. Jesus answered, "You say that I am a king. In fact, the reason I was born and came into the world is to testify to the truth. Everyone on the side of truth listens to me." JOHN 18:37 NIV

This is good and pleases God our Savior, who wants everyone to be saved and to understand the truth. 1 TIMOTHY 2:3–4 NLT

But you have received the Holy Spirit, and he lives within you, so you don't need anyone to teach you what is true. For the Spirit teaches you everything you need to know, and what he teaches is true—it is not a lie. So just as he has taught you, remain in fellowship with Christ. 1 JOHN 2:27 NLT

This is He who came by water and blood—Jesus Christ; not only by water, but by water and blood. And it is the Spirit who bears witness, because the Spirit is truth. 1 JOHN 5:6 NKJV

...it is *the Spirit* who bears witness, because *the Spirit is truth.*

Understanding

(awareness; comprehension)

My son, if you receive my words, And treasure my commands within you, So that you incline your ear to wisdom, *And* apply your heart to understanding; Yes, if you cry out for discernment, *And* lift up your voice for understanding, If you seek her as silver, And search for her as *for* hidden treasures; Then you will understand the fear of the LORD, And find the knowledge of God. For the LORD gives wisdom; From His mouth *come* knowledge and understanding; He stores up sound wisdom for the upright; He is a shield to those who walk uprightly; He guards the paths of justice, And preserves the way of His saints. Then you will understand righteousness and justice, Equity *and* every good path. **PROVERBS 2:1–9 NKJV**

Then he added, "Pay close attention to what you hear. The closer you listen, the more understanding you will be given—and you will receive even more. To those who listen to my teaching, more understanding will be given. But for those who are not listening, even what little understanding they have will be taken away from them." **MARK 4:24–25 NLT**

These are the things God has revealed to us by his Spirit. The Spirit searches all things, even the deep things of God. For who knows a person's thoughts except their own spirit within them? In the same way no one knows the thoughts of God except the Spirit of God. What we have received is not the spirit of the world, but the Spirit who is from God, so that we may understand what God has freely given us. **1 CORINTHIANS 2:10–12 NIV**

He has showered his kindness on us, along with all wisdom and understanding. God has now revealed to us his mysterious plan regarding Christ, a plan to fulfill his own good pleasure. And this is the plan: At the right time he will bring everything together under the authority of Christ—everything in heaven and on earth. EPHESIANS 1:8–10 NLT

So we have not stopped praying for you since we first heard about you. We ask God to give you complete knowledge of his will and to give you spiritual wisdom and understanding. COLOSSIANS 1:9 NLT

Do your best to improve your faith. You can do this by adding goodness, understanding, self-control, patience, devotion to God, concern for others, and love. If you keep growing in this way, it will show that what you know about our Lord Jesus Christ has made your lives useful and meaningful. 2 PETER 1:5–8 CEV

And we know that the Son of God has come, and he has given us understanding so that we can know the true God. And now we live in fellowship with the true God because we live in fellowship with his Son, Jesus Christ. He is the only true God, and he is eternal life. 1 JOHN 5:20 NLT

Victory

(triumph; overcoming of obstacles)

The LORD will grant that the enemies who rise up against you will be defeated before you. They will come at you from one direction but flee from you in seven . . . The LORD will make you the head, not the tail. If you pay attention to the commands of the LORD your God that I give you this day and carefully follow them, you will always be at the top, never at the bottom. DEUTERONOMY 28:7, 13 NIV

"The LORD your God is with you, the Mighty Warrior who saves. He will take great delight in you; in his love he will no longer rebuke you, but will rejoice over you with singing." ZEPHANIAH 3:17 NIV

If God is for us, who can be against us? . . . Who shall separate us from the love of Christ? Shall trouble or hardship or persecution or famine or nakedness or danger or sword? . . . No, in all these things we are more than conquerors through him who loved us. For I am convinced that neither death nor life, neither angels nor demons, neither the present nor the future, nor any powers, neither height nor depth, nor anything else in all creation, will be able to separate us from the love of God that is in Christ Jesus our Lord. ROMANS 8:31, 35, 37–39 NIV

But thank God! He gives us victory over sin and death through our Lord Jesus Christ. 1 CORINTHIANS 15:57 NLT

But you belong to God, my dear children. You have already won a victory over those people, because the Spirit who lives in you is greater than the spirit who lives in the world. 1 JOHN 4:4 NLT

Everyone who believes that Jesus is the Christ is born of God, and everyone who loves the father loves his child as well. This is how we know that we love the children of God: by loving God and carrying out his commands. In fact, this is love for God: to keep his commands. And his commands are not burdensome, for everyone born of God overcomes the world. This is the victory that has overcome the world, even our faith. Who is it that overcomes the world? Only he who believes that Jesus is the Son of God. 1 JOHN 5:1–5 NIV

This is the *victory*
that has *overcome the world,*
even our faith.

❧ Day 98 ❧

Vindication

(to defend)

"For the LORD will vindicate His people, And will have compassion on His servants, When He sees that *their* strength is gone, And there is none *remaining*, bond or free." DEUTERONOMY 32:36 NASB

Then the Cushite arrived and said, "My lord the king, hear the good news! The Lord has vindicated you today by delivering you from the hand of all who rose up against you." 2 SAMUEL 18:31 NIV

"Pay attention, Job, and listen to me; be silent, and I will speak. If you have anything to say, answer me; speak up, for I want to vindicate you. But if not, then listen to me; be silent, and I will teach you wisdom." JOB 33:31-33 NIV

Hear me, LORD, my plea is just; listen to my cry. Hear my prayer—it does not rise from deceitful lips. Let my vindication come from you; may your eyes see what is right. Though you probe my heart, though you examine me at night and test me, you will find that I have planned no evil; my mouth has not transgressed. PSALM 17:1-3 NIV

They will receive blessing from the LORD and vindication from God their Savior. PSALM 24:5 NIV

For the LORD will vindicate his people and have compassion on his servants. PSALM 135:14 NIV

He who vindicates me is near. Who then will bring charges against me? Let us face each other! Who is my accuser? Let him confront me! ISAIAH 50:8 NIV

"No weapon that is formed against you will prosper; And every tongue that accuses you in judgment you will condemn. This is the heritage of the servants of the LORD, And their vindication is from Me," declares the LORD. ISAIAH 54:17 NASB

The Son of Man will send his angels, and they will remove from his Kingdom everything that causes sin and all who do evil. And the angels will throw them into the fiery furnace, where there will be weeping and gnashing of teeth. Then the righteous will shine like the sun in their Father's Kingdom. Anyone with ears to hear should listen and understand! MATTHEW 13:41–43 NLT

Then the righteous
will shine like the sun
in their *Father's Kingdom.*

Wisdom

*(power of judging rightly based on knowledge,
experience, and understanding)*

Solomon said to God, "You have dealt with my father David with great lovingkindness, and have made me king in his place. Now, O LORD God, Your promise to my father David is fulfilled, for You have made me king over a people as numerous as the dust of the earth. Give me now wisdom and knowledge, that I may go out and come in before this people, for who can rule this great people of Yours?" God said to Solomon, "Because you had this in mind, and did not ask for riches, wealth or honor, or the life of those who hate you, nor have you even asked for long life, but you have asked for yourself wisdom and knowledge that you may rule My people over whom I have made you king, wisdom and knowledge have been granted to you. And I will give you riches and wealth and honor, such as none of the kings who were before you has possessed nor those who will come after you." So Solomon went from the high place which was at Gibeon, from the tent of meeting, to Jerusalem, and he reigned over Israel. 2 CHRONICLES 1:8–13 NASB

God gives wisdom, knowledge, and joy to those who please him. ECCLESIASTES 2:26 NLT

Wisdom belongs to the aged, and understanding to the old. "But true wisdom and power are found in God; counsel and understanding are his." JOB 12:12–13 NLT

. . . and said: "Praise be to the name of God for ever and ever; wisdom and power are his. He changes times and seasons; he deposes kings and raises up others. He gives wisdom to the wise and knowledge to the discerning. He reveals deep and hidden things; he knows what lies in darkness, and light dwells with him. I thank and praise you, God of my ancestors: You have given me wisdom and power, you have made known to me what we asked of you, you have made known to us the dream of the king." DANIEL 2:20–23 NIV

Oh, how great are God's riches and wisdom and knowledge! How impossible it is for us to understand his decisions and his ways! For who can know the LORD's thoughts? Who knows enough to give him advice? And who has given him so much that he needs to pay it back? For everything comes from him and exists by his power and is intended for his glory. All glory to him forever! Amen. ROMANS 11:33–36 NLT

If you need wisdom, ask our generous God, and he will give it to you. He will not rebuke you for asking. JAMES 1:5 NLT

If you need *wisdom*,
ask our generous God,
and *he will give it to you.*

❧ Day 100 ❧

Words

(utterance; communication; statement or expression)

"Behold, I will pour out my spirit on you; I will make my words known to you." PROVERBS 1:23 NASB

When you are arrested, don't worry about how to respond or what to say. God will give you the right words at the right time. MATTHEW 10:19 NLT

Heaven and earth will pass away, but my words will never pass away. MATTHEW 24:35 NIV

Whenever you are arrested and brought to trial, do not worry beforehand about what to say. Just say whatever is given you at the time, for it is not you speaking, but the Holy Spirit. MARK 13:11 NIV

One day Jesus was praying in a certain place. When he finished, one of his disciples said to him, "Lord, teach us to pray, just as John taught his disciples." He said to them, "When you pray, say: 'Father, hallowed be your name, your kingdom come. Give us each day our daily bread. Forgive us our sins, for we also forgive everyone who sins against us. And lead us not into temptation.'" LUKE 11:1–4 NIV

But before all this, they will seize you and persecute you. They will hand you over to synagogues and put you in prison, and you will be brought before kings and governors, and all on account of my name. And so you will bear testimony to me. But make up your mind not to worry beforehand how you will defend yourselves. For

I will give you words and wisdom that none of your adversaries will be able to resist or contradict. LUKE 21:12–15 NIV

For I gave them the words you gave me and they accepted them. They knew with certainty that I came from you, and they believed that you sent me. JOHN 17:8 NIV

And the Holy Spirit helps us in our weakness. For example, we don't know what God wants us to pray for. But the Holy Spirit prays for us with groanings that cannot be expressed in words. And the Father who knows all hearts knows what the Spirit is saying, for the Spirit pleads for us believers in harmony with God's own will. ROMANS 8:26–27 NLT

When we tell you these things, we do not use words that come from human wisdom. Instead, we speak words given to us by the Spirit, using the Spirit's words to explain spiritual truths.
1 CORINTHIANS 2:13 NLT

And pray for me, too. Ask God to give me the right words so I can boldly explain God's mysterious plan that the Good News is for Jews and Gentiles alike. I am in chains now, still preaching this message as God's ambassador. So pray that I will keep on speaking boldly for him, as I should. EPHESIANS 6:19–20 NLT